The Children's
Dinosaur
ENCYCLOPEDIA

The Children's
Dinosaur
ENCYCLOPEDIA

CONSULTANT: PROFESSOR MICHAEL J. BENTON

NEW BURLINGTON BOOKS

A Marshall Edition
Conceived, edited, and designed by
Marshall Editions

First published in 2002 by
New Burlington Books
6 Blundell Street
London
N7 9BH

This edition published in 2005

Originated in Singapore by HBM Print
Printed and bound in Thailand by Imago

Author: Jinny Johnson
Consultant: Professor Michael J. Benton,
Department of Earth Sciences,
University of Bristol, England

Designer: Nelupa Hussain
Design Manager: Ralph Pitchford
Art Director: Simon Webb
Managing Editor: Kate Phelps
Proofreader: Lindsay McTeague
Editorial Director: Cynthia O'Brien
Picture Research: Zilda Tandy
Production: James Bann

Pelecanimimus

Contents

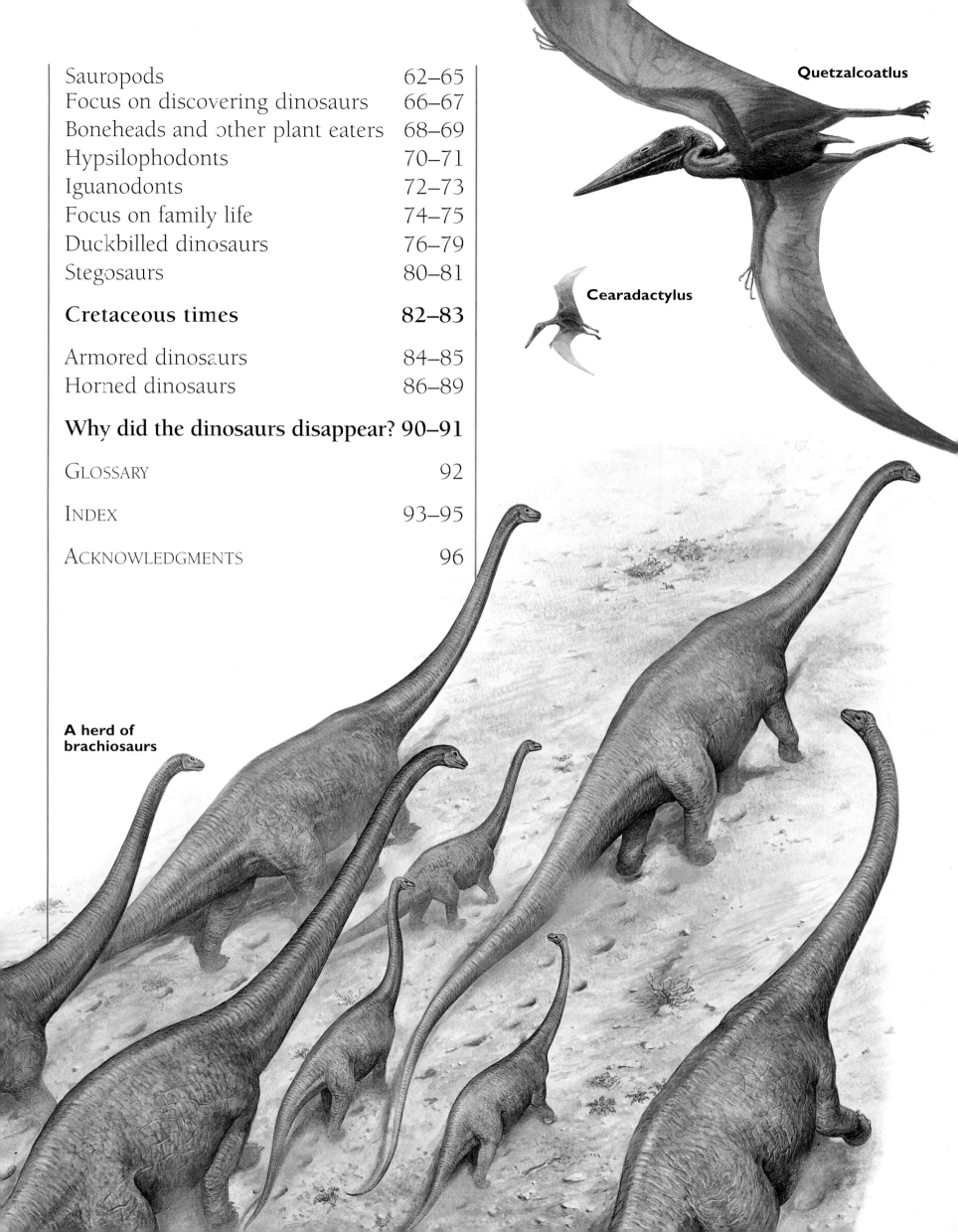

Quetzalcoatlus

Cearadactylus

A herd of brachiosaurs

Introduction

The Earth is about 4.6 billion years old and the first signs of life on our planet date back at least 3.5 billion years. This book looks at one of the most exciting times in the history of life on the Earth: the development of the first true land animals, the reptiles, and their most amazing representatives, the dinosaurs. Despite the fact that most of the creatures in this book became extinct millions of years before the first humans lived, dinosaurs and their relatives are among the most fascinating of all creatures. This encyclopedia aims to bring them to life again and present them as the living, breathing animals they once were.

Our changing world

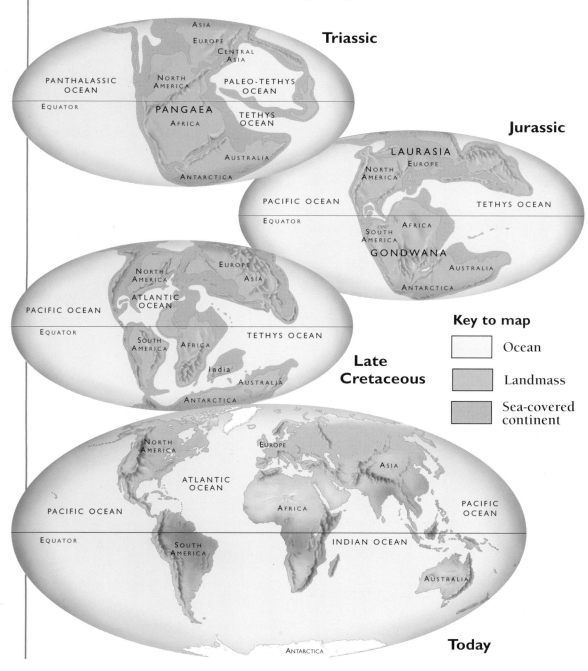

Key to map

☐ Ocean

▨ Landmass

▨ Sea-covered continent

Plates colliding

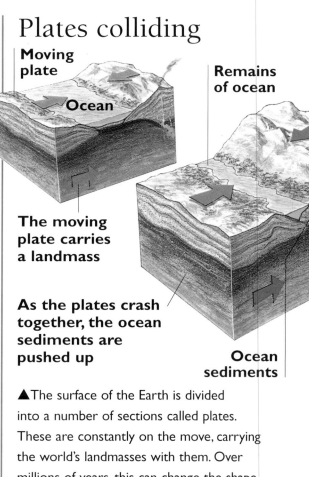

▲The surface of the Earth is divided into a number of sections called plates. These are constantly on the move, carrying the world's landmasses with them. Over millions of years, this can change the shape of continents as happened during the time of the dinosaurs. When one plate collides with another, land and ocean sediments can be pushed up, creating a mountain range.

◀This series of maps shows how the shape of the Earth's landmasses has changed over millions of years. During the Triassic, when dinosaurs first appeared, most of the world's land formed one supercontinent called Pangaea. During the Jurassic, Pangaea started to split apart, forming northern and southern landmasses. By the Late Cretaceous, these had subdivided further and were beginning to take the shape of the continents we know today.

▶The history of the Earth is divided into two major eons: the Precambrian and the Phanerozoic. The Precambrian is the largest, spanning the time from the Earth's origins to the beginnings of life. The Phanerozoic dates from the time when life began to thrive on the Earth and includes three eras: the Paleozoic, Mesozoic, and Cenozoic. These are in turn divided into periods and epochs. The dates on the chart show how many millions of years ago (mya) each began.

How to use this book

This encyclopedia is divided into two chapters: early reptiles and dinosaurs. Each chapter contains an introduction, a description of what makes a reptile or a dinosaur, illustrations of and facts about different species, and focus pages that look in more detail at particular topics. There are also special double-page features on the three periods in the age of the dinosaurs—the Triassic, Jurassic, and Cretaceous—and one on why dinosaurs disappeared.

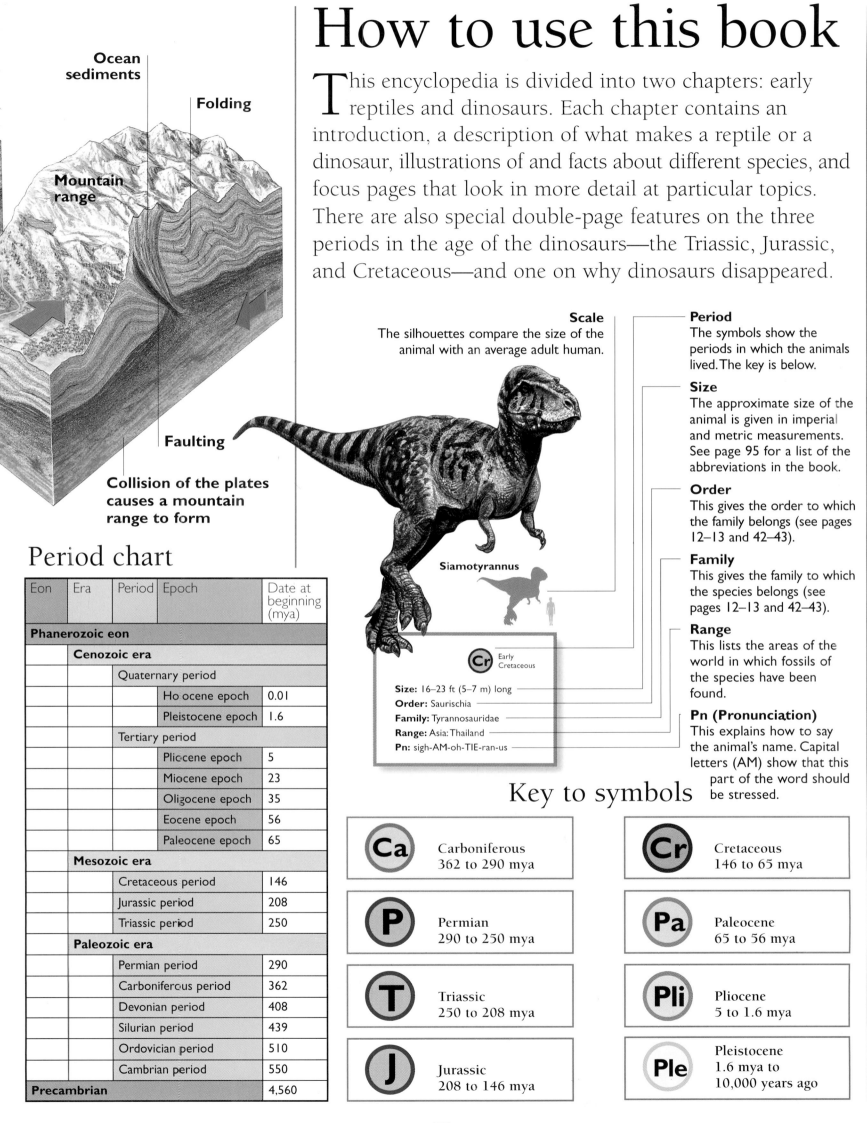

Ocean sediments

Folding

Mountain range

Faulting

Collision of the plates causes a mountain range to form

Scale
The silhouettes compare the size of the animal with an average adult human.

Siamotyrannus

Cr Early Cretaceous

Size: 16–23 ft (5–7 m) long
Order: Saurischia
Family: Tyrannosauridae
Range: Asia: Thailand
Pn: sigh-AM-oh-TIE-ran-us

Period
The symbols show the periods in which the animals lived. The key is below.

Size
The approximate size of the animal is given in imperial and metric measurements. See page 95 for a list of the abbreviations in the book.

Order
This gives the order to which the family belongs (see pages 12–13 and 42–43).

Family
This gives the family to which the species belongs (see pages 12–13 and 42–43).

Range
This lists the areas of the world in which fossils of the species have been found.

Pn (Pronunciation)
This explains how to say the animal's name. Capital letters (AM) show that this part of the word should be stressed.

Period chart

Eon	Era	Period	Epoch	Date at beginning (mya)
Phanerozoic eon				
	Cenozoic era			
		Quaternary period		
			Holocene epoch	0.01
			Pleistocene epoch	1.6
		Tertiary period		
			Pliocene epoch	5
			Miocene epoch	23
			Oligocene epoch	35
			Eocene epoch	56
			Paleocene epoch	65
	Mesozoic era			
		Cretaceous period		146
		Jurassic period		208
		Triassic period		250
	Paleozoic era			
		Permian period		290
		Carboniferous period		362
		Devonian period		408
		Silurian period		439
		Ordovician period		510
		Cambrian period		550
Precambrian				4,560

Key to symbols

Ca Carboniferous 362 to 290 mya

P Permian 290 to 250 mya

T Triassic 250 to 208 mya

J Jurassic 208 to 146 mya

Cr Cretaceous 146 to 65 mya

Pa Paleocene 65 to 56 mya

Pli Pliocene 5 to 1.6 mya

Ple Pleistocene 1.6 mya to 10,000 years ago

Early Reptiles

Reptiles today include animals such as turtles, crocodiles, lizards, and snakes. All have a bony skeleton and scaly skin, and most lay eggs. Although turtles and a few other kinds of reptiles live in water, most spend their lives on land.

In prehistoric times there were many kinds of reptiles not found today. The first reptiles, which lived 100 million years before the dinosaurs, were small lizardlike creatures. Later, at the time of the dinosaurs, came the flying reptiles called pterosaurs and the many kinds of marine reptiles such as ichthyosaurs and plesiosaurs. Another important group included the mammal-like reptiles, which dominated life on the Earth before the dinosaurs but died out by the end of the Jurassic period. The most complex of these reptiles were the ancestors of the mammals, the group to which humans belong.

This fossilized skull belonged to a flying reptile called **Scaphognathus**, which lived in Europe during the Jurassic period. It probably fed on fish, swooping down to snatch its prey from the water in its long jaws.

Longisquama

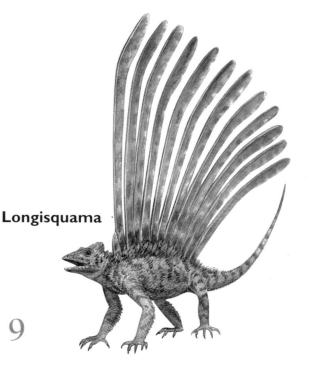

What were the early reptiles?

Reptiles developed from amphibians and were the first true land vertebrates (animals with backbones). Amphibians generally lay their eggs in water and spend the first part of their lives there. The great advance of the reptiles was that they had an egg with a shell that did not dry out in air and could be laid on dry land, so freeing them from their dependence on water. After the appearance of the first reptiles in the Late Carboniferous, different types of reptiles began to spread all over the world. At the same time, marine forms such as plesiosaurs and ichthyosaurs were beginning to thrive in the sea. Crocodiles and flying reptiles belonged to the archosaur or "ruling reptile" group, as did the dinosaurs. Of these, only crocodiles remain today.

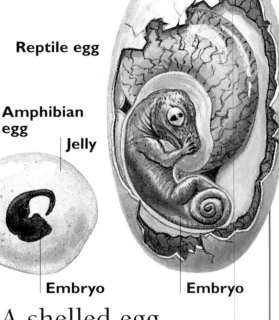

Shell

Reptile egg

Amphibian egg

Jelly

Embryo

Embryo

A shelled egg

An amphibian egg is protected only by a jelly coating. The egg of a reptile is protected by a tough shell, which keeps the developing baby, called an embryo, from drying out. It also protects it from predators.

An early reptile

One of the first reptiles and earliest of all land vertebrates, *Hylonomus* was a lightly built, lizardlike creature. Its jaws were more powerful than those of its amphibian ancestors and its hips and shoulders were stronger to help support it on land.

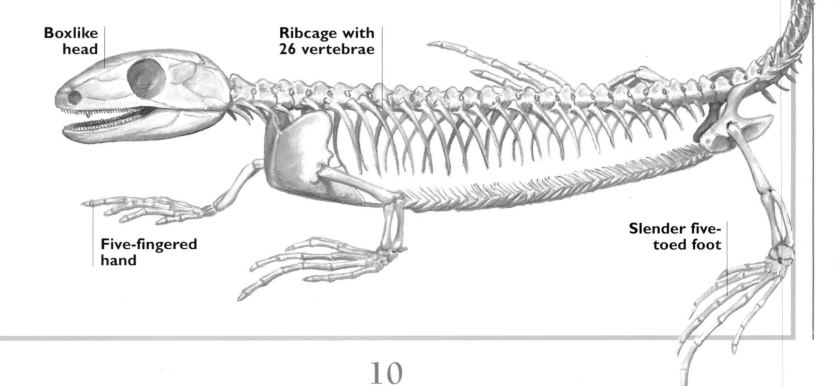

Long bony tail

SKELETON OF A HYLONOMUS

Boxlike head

Ribcage with 26 vertebrae

Five-fingered hand

Slender five-toed foot

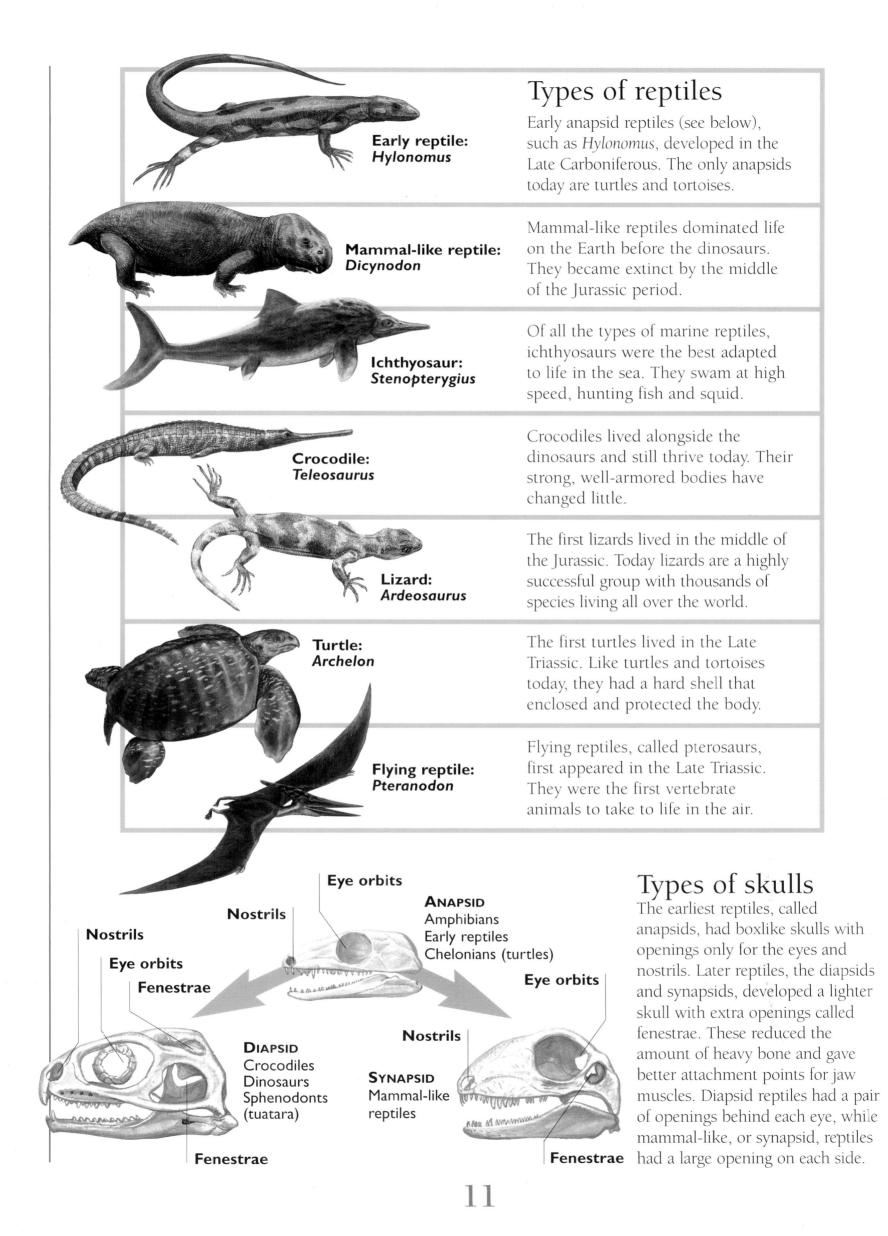

Types of reptiles

Early reptile:
Hylonomus

Early anapsid reptiles (see below), such as *Hylonomus*, developed in the Late Carboniferous. The only anapsids today are turtles and tortoises.

Mammal-like reptile:
Dicynodon

Mammal-like reptiles dominated life on the Earth before the dinosaurs. They became extinct by the middle of the Jurassic period.

Ichthyosaur:
Stenopterygius

Of all the types of marine reptiles, ichthyosaurs were the best adapted to life in the sea. They swam at high speed, hunting fish and squid.

Crocodile:
Teleosaurus

Crocodiles lived alongside the dinosaurs and still thrive today. Their strong, well-armored bodies have changed little.

Lizard:
Ardeosaurus

The first lizards lived in the middle of the Jurassic. Today lizards are a highly successful group with thousands of species living all over the world.

Turtle:
Archelon

The first turtles lived in the Late Triassic. Like turtles and tortoises today, they had a hard shell that enclosed and protected the body.

Flying reptile:
Pteranodon

Flying reptiles, called pterosaurs, first appeared in the Late Triassic. They were the first vertebrate animals to take to life in the air.

Eye orbits

Nostrils

ANAPSID
Amphibians
Early reptiles
Chelonians (turtles)

Nostrils

Eye orbits

Fenestrae

Eye orbits

DIAPSID
Crocodiles
Dinosaurs
Sphenodonts
(tuatara)

Nostrils

SYNAPSID
Mammal-like
reptiles

Fenestrae

Fenestrae

Types of skulls

The earliest reptiles, called anapsids, had boxlike skulls with openings only for the eyes and nostrils. Later reptiles, the diapsids and synapsids, developed a lighter skull with extra openings called fenestrae. These reduced the amount of heavy bone and gave better attachment points for jaw muscles. Diapsid reptiles had a pair of openings behind each eye, while mammal-like, or synapsid, reptiles had a large opening on each side.

11

A reptile family tree

The first reptiles, which appeared in the Late Carboniferous, were the primitive anapsids, still represented today by tortoises and turtles. They gave rise to the synapsid reptiles, the ancestors of the mammals, and to the diapsid reptiles, which later included dinosaurs as well as modern lizards and snakes. Many of these groups of reptiles are now extinct.

Reptile groups

Animals are classified into groups of different sizes. The smallest is the species, and every species is contained in a genus (plural, genera). So for *Pterodactylus kochi*, *kochi* is the species name and *Pterodactylus* the genus. All genera are classified into families, families into suborders, suborders into orders, and so on.

SYNAPSIDA

ANAPSIDA

REPTILES

DIAPSIDA

ARCHOSAUR-OMORPHA

The chart

At the far right of the chart the names ending in "idae" are all families, which contain a number of closely related species of reptiles. Names ending in "ia" or "formes" are larger groups, containing a number of families. Names in capital letters are of major groups such as mammals and dinosaurs. The orders and suborders (such as Archosauria) in the book are also labeled.

Two **paleontologists** work on a reconstructed skeleton of a plesiosaur, a type of marine reptile common at the time of the dinosaurs. Experts have long argued about how these reptiles moved. At first, they thought that they beat their paddlelike flippers backwards and forwards like oars. Now most agree that plesiosaurs moved their paddles in a figure-eight shape as though flying through the water.

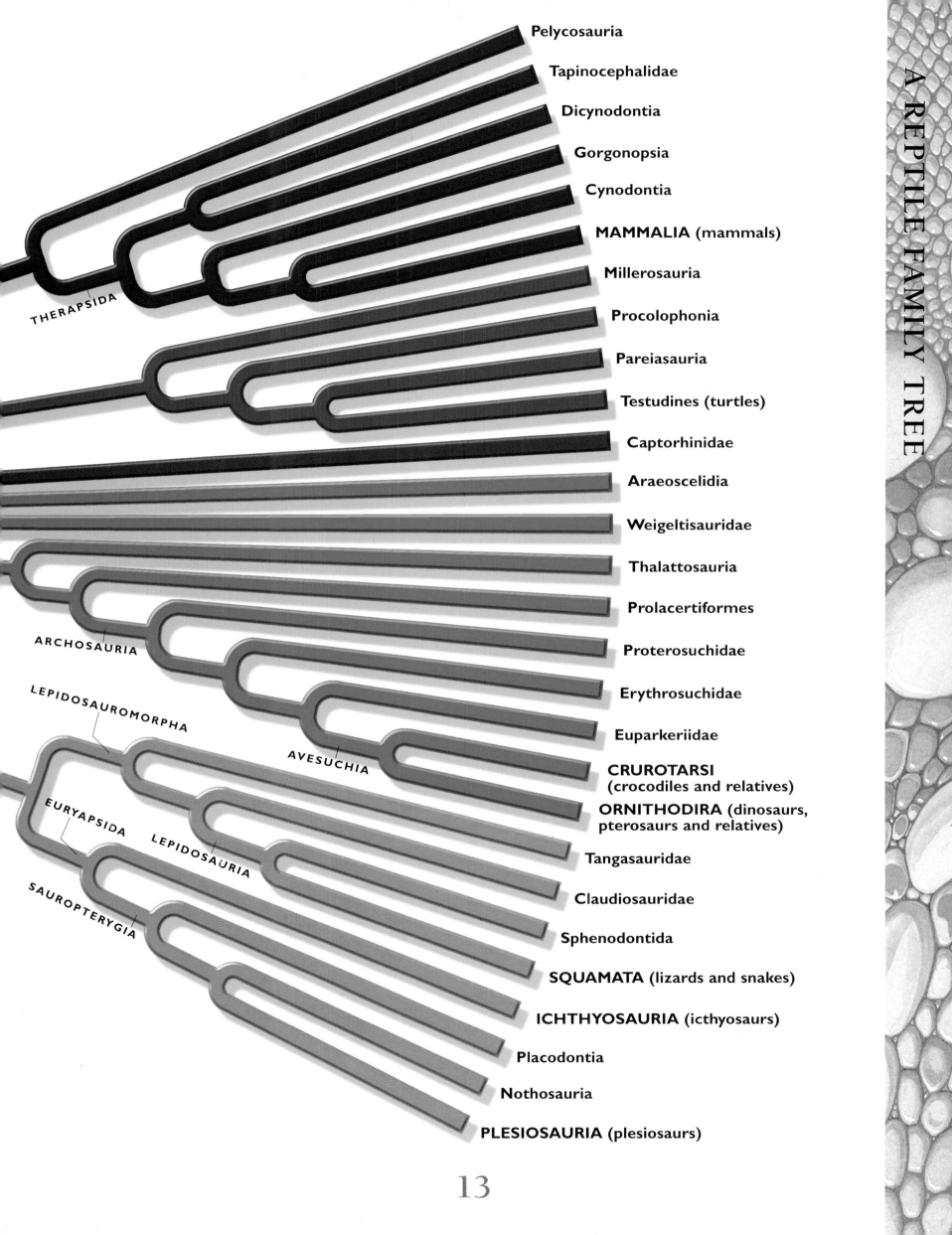

Pelycosauria

Tapinocephalidae

Dicynodontia

Gorgonopsia

Cynodontia

MAMMALIA (mammals)

Millerosauria

Procolophonia

Pareiasauria

Testudines (turtles)

Captorhinidae

Araeoscelidia

Weigeltisauridae

Thalattosauria

Prolacertiformes

Proterosuchidae

Erythrosuchidae

Euparkeriidae

CRUROTARSI
(crocodiles and relatives)

ORNITHODIRA (dinosaurs,
pterosaurs and relatives)

Tangasauridae

Claudiosauridae

Sphenodontida

SQUAMATA (lizards and snakes)

ICHTHYOSAURIA (icthyosaurs)

Placodontia

Nothosauria

PLESIOSAURIA (plesiosaurs)

THERAPSIDA

ARCHOSAURIA

LEPIDOSAUROMORPHA

AVESUCHIA

EURYAPSIDA

LEPIDOSAURIA

SAUROPTERYGIA

A REPTILE FAMILY TREE

13

The first reptiles

Reptiles evolved during the Late Carboniferous period about 300 million years ago. Many groups thrived before the archosaurs, or ruling reptiles, which included dinosaurs, began to dominate. The earliest, most primitive reptiles, called anapsids, had one feature in common—the skull was a heavy box of bone with no openings other than for the eyes and nostrils. Because the jaw muscles were inside the skull, they were not very big and this meant that the mouth could not be opened very wide. Later reptiles, or diapsids, had a pair of openings, called fenestrae, either side of the skull behind the eye. The jaw muscles stretched across these holes, allowing the jaws to be opened wider.

Longisquama

A curious, lizardlike creature, *Longisquama* had a row of tall V-shaped scales rising from its back. Some experts believe that when these were held out at the animal's sides, they might have allowed it to glide short distances through the air, like gliding lizards today.

(P) Late Permian

Size: 24 in (60 cm) long
Order: Millerosauria
Family: Millerettidae
Range: Africa: South Africa
Pn: MILL-er-ETT-ah

(T) Early Triassic

Size: 6 in (15 cm) long
Order: Prolacertiformes
Family: Longisquamidae
Range: Asia
Pn: LONG-ih-SQUAM-a

Milleretta

Hylonomus

The remains of *Hylonomus,* one of the earliest reptiles known, have been found in the fossilized trunks of club moss trees. Floods buried the lower part of the trunks in mud, causing the trees to die and their interiors to rot away. Insects that gathered inside the trunks attracted *Hylonomus.* Once inside, the reptiles were unable to escape and were eventually fossilized.

Milleretta

This small lizardlike creature was fast-moving and probably fed on insects. So far millerettids have only been found from the Late Permian period in South Africa. Although its skull did have openings on either side, *Milleretta* was a primitive anapsid reptile.

Longisquama

(Ca) Middle Carboniferous

Size: 8 in (20 cm) long
Order: Captorhinidae
Family: Protorothyrididae
Range: North America: Nova Scotia
Pn: HY-lo-NOME-us

Hylonomus

14

Pareiasaurus

Pareiasaurus

The largest of the early reptiles, pareiasaurs grew to lengths of up to 10 feet (3 m). *Pareiasaurus* was typical, with its heavy body and back protected by plates of bone set into the skin. A plant eater, it had small teeth with serrated edges for chopping tough leaves.

P Micdle Permian

Size: 8 ft (2.5 m) long
Order: Pareiasauria
Family: Pareiasauridae
Range: Africa; eastern Europe
Pn: par-EYE-ah-SAW-rus

Petrolacosaurus

One cf the first diapsid reptiles, *Petrolacosaurus* had a slender lizardlike body. It had longer legs than a typical lizard and its tail was as long as its head and body combined. It probably chased insects to eat, snapping them up in its small sharp teeth.

Askeptosaurus

Askeptosaurus belonged to a family of diapsid reptiles known as thalattosaurs, which were adapted for life in the sea. It had a slender body, an extremely long tail and broad webbed feet. The long jaws were lined with many sharp teeth, ideal for catching fish.

T Triassic

Size: 16 in (40 cm) long
Order: Thalattosauria
Family: Askeptosauridae
Range: Europe: Switzerland
Pn: a-SKEPT-o-SAW-rus

Askeptosaurus

Petrolacosaurus

Ca Late Carbonifercus

Size: 16 in (40 cm) long
Order: Araeoscelidia
Family: Petrolacosauridae
Range: North America: Kansas
Pn: PET-rol-AK-oh-SAW-rus

T Late Triassic

Size: 13 in (33 cm) long
Order: Procolophonia
Family: Procolophonidae
Range: North America: New Jersey
Pn: HIP-sog-NAY-thus

Hypsognathus

Among the earliest reptiles were the procolophonids, which lived until the Late Triassic. *Hypsognathus* was one of the later members of the family. It had a wide squat body and was probably not a fast runner. The spikes around its head would have helped protect it from any enemies.

Hypsognathus

15

Mammal-like reptiles

The first of these reptiles lived some 300 million years ago and dominated the Earth until the appearance of the dinosaurs in the Triassic. Pelycosaurs, the earliest group, lived in the Late Carboniferous and Early Permian. They rapidly evolved from small lizardlike creatures into animals of a heavier build with strong jaws and teeth of different shapes. Later, during the Permian, came several more advanced groups, such as the plant-eating dicynodonts, the carnivorous gorgonopsians, and the cynodonts. The cynodonts were the most advanced mammal-like reptiles and survived the longest. Among them were the direct ancestors of mammals, the dominant land animals today.

T Early Triassic

Size: 3¼ ft (1 m) long
Suborder: Cynodontia
Family: Cynognathidae
Range: Africa: South Africa; South America: Argentina
Pn: SIGH-nog-NAY-thus

Cynognathus

Cynognathus

One of the largest cynodonts, *Cynognathus* had a powerful body and a head that was more than 12 inches (30 cm) long. Its strong jaws show that it was a fierce hunter. Like mammals, it had three types of teeth: cutting incisor teeth, stabbing canines, and larger cheek teeth for chewing.

Edaphosaurus

P Early Permian

Size: 10 ft (3 m) long
Order: Pelycosauria
Family: Edaphosauridae
Range: Europe; North America: Texas
Pn: ee-daph-o-SAW-rus

Edaphosaurus

On its back, *Edaphosaurus* had long spines, which were probably covered with skin rich in blood vessels. This sail-like structure may have helped to control its temperature. The pelycosaur might have turned toward the sun to warm the blood as it flowed through the skin on the sail, and away from the sun and into the wind to cool down.

Kannemeyeria

A plant-eating reptile with a huge head, *Kannemeyeria* was one of the biggest of the dicynodonts. Strong heavy limbs supported the bulky body. It could have used its hard beak to tear up mouthfuls of leaves and roots, which it then ground down in its toothless jaws.

T Middle Triassic

Size: 10 ft (3 m) long
Suborder: Dicynodontia
Family: Kannemeyeriidae
Range: Africa: South Africa; Asia: India; South America: Argentina
Pn: KAN-eh-MAY-er-ee-a

Kannemeyeria

16

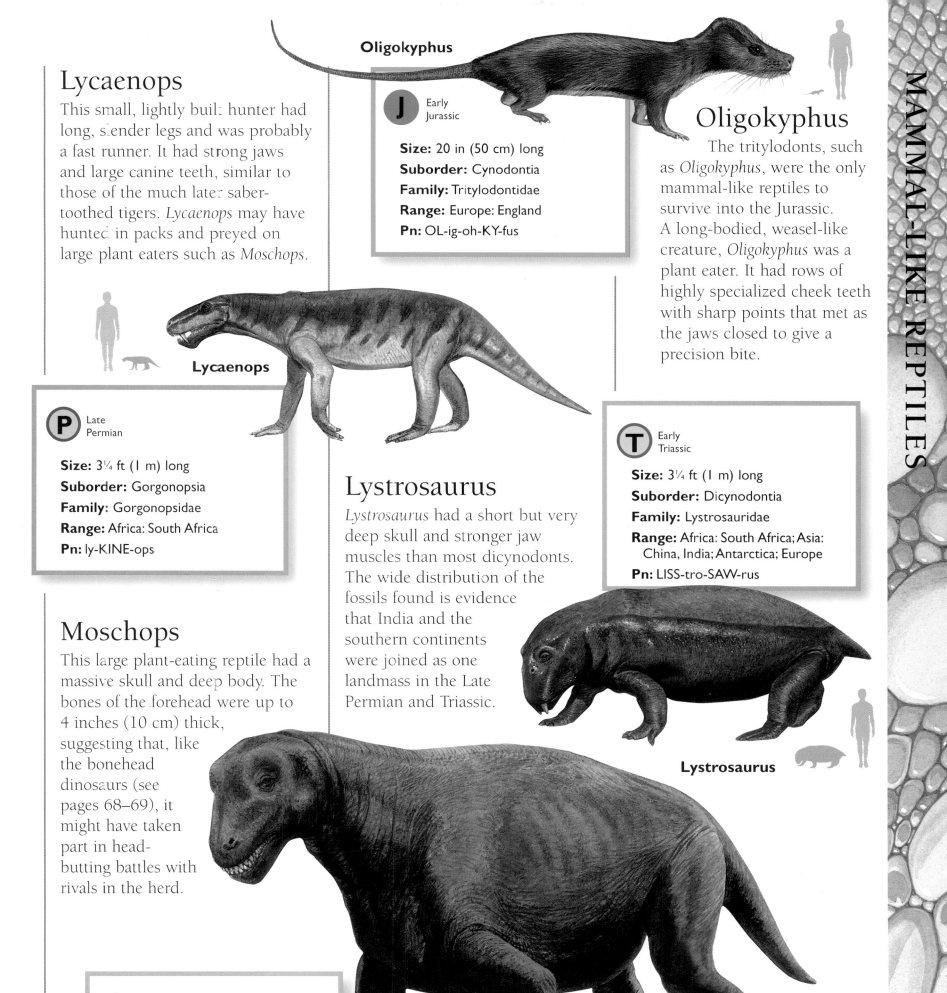

Lycaenops

This small, lightly built hunter had long, slender legs and was probably a fast runner. It had strong jaws and large canine teeth, similar to those of the much later saber-toothed tigers. *Lycaenops* may have hunted in packs and preyed on large plant eaters such as *Moschops*.

Lycaenops

P Late Permian

Size: 3¼ ft (1 m) long
Suborder: Gorgonopsia
Family: Gorgonopsidae
Range: Africa: South Africa
Pn: ly-KINE-ops

Moschops

This large plant-eating reptile had a massive skull and deep body. The bones of the forehead were up to 4 inches (10 cm) thick, suggesting that, like the bonehead dinosaurs (see pages 68–69), it might have taken part in head-butting battles with rivals in the herd.

P Late Permian

Size: 16 ft (5 m) long
Order: Therapsida
Family: Tapinocephalidae
Range: Africa: South Africa
Pn: MOS-chops

Moschops

Oligokyphus

J Early Jurassic

Size: 20 in (50 cm) long
Suborder: Cynodontia
Family: Tritylodontidae
Range: Europe: England
Pn: OL-ig-oh-KY-fus

Oligokyphus

The tritylodonts, such as *Oligokyphus*, were the only mammal-like reptiles to survive into the Jurassic. A long-bodied, weasel-like creature, *Oligokyphus* was a plant eater. It had rows of highly specialized cheek teeth with sharp points that met as the jaws closed to give a precision bite.

Lystrosaurus

Lystrosaurus had a short but very deep skull and stronger jaw muscles than most dicynodonts. The wide distribution of the fossils found is evidence that India and the southern continents were joined as one landmass in the Late Permian and Triassic.

T Early Triassic

Size: 3¼ ft (1 m) long
Suborder: Dicynodontia
Family: Lystrosauridae
Range: Africa: South Africa; Asia: China, India; Antarctica; Europe
Pn: LISS-tro-SAW-rus

Lystrosaurus

Triassic times

When the Triassic period began about 250 million years ago, life on the Earth was dominated by mammal-like reptiles, as well by other reptiles such as crocodiles. Frogs, turtles, and fish swam in rivers, and in the seas were marine reptiles such as ichthyosaurs and nothosaurs. Toward the end of the Triassic the first dinosaurs appeared and quickly spread across Pangaea. Many of the earlier reptiles had died out by the time the dinosaurs became the dominant large animals.

Triassic Germany

This scene in what is now southern Germany shows a group of plant-eating dinosaurs browsing on conifer branches. They are disturbed by the arrival of a predatory ceratosaur *Liliensternus*. Small crocodiles, *Terrestrisuchus*, and shrewlike mammals feed on insects in the tangled undergrowth of cycads and horsetails, while pterosaurs soar overhead.

Eudimorphodon, a flying reptile (pterosaur)

Liliensternus, a ceratosaur

Terrestrisuchus, a crocodile

Dragonfly

Fern

The Triassic world

In the Triassic period the continents were all joined in one supercontinent, known as Pangaea, which lay across the Equator. This meant that the animals and plants of the time were able to spread across the world with ease. The climate was generally warm, with little variation, and there were no polar ice caps.

Asia

Europe

Germany

China

Central Asia

PANTHALASSIC OCEAN

North America

PALEO-TETHYS OCEAN

EQUATOR

PANGAEA

Africa

TETHYS OCEAN

India

Australia

Antarctica

Key to map

Ocean

Landmass

Sea-covered continent

Plateosaurus, a prosauropod

Peteinosaurus, a flying reptile (pterosaur)

Conifers

Thecodontosaurus, a prosauropod

Cycad

Shrewlike mammal

Moss

Turtles, tortoises, and terrapins

Turtles and their relatives first appeared in the Late Triassic more than 200 million years ago. Even then, a typical turtle had a hard shell enclosing its body and probably looked remarkably like the turtles and tortoises of today. Like them, many of the prehistoric turtles could pull their head and legs into the shell for protection from enemies. The shell covering the back was made of bony plates, covered with a layer of smooth horn—like the "tortoise shell" from which combs and other accessories used to be made. Bony plates protected the underside. Like turtles and tortoises today, most early forms of turtles and tortoises had toothless jaws and a hard beak made of horn for cropping plants.

Proganochelys

T Late Triassic

Size: 3¼ ft (1 m) long
Order: Testudines
Family: Proganochelyidae
Range: Europe: Germany
Pn: PRO-gan-oh-KEEL-is

Proganochelys

This is one of the earliest turtles known. It had a broad, domed shell covering its back and bony plates protected its soft underside. It also had a number of extra plates around the edges of its shell, which gave the legs some protection. *Proganochelys* did have some teeth in its mouth, but it also had a toothless, horn-covered beak like that of today's turtles.

Archelon

Archelon

This giant turtle did not have the heavy shell typical of most of its land and freshwater relatives. Instead, its body was protected by a framework of bony struts, which were probably covered by a thick layer of rubbery skin. Its limbs were massive paddles that it used to propel itself through water. Like modern leatherback turtles, *Archelon* may have fed on jellyfish.

Cr Late Cretaceous

Size: 12 ft (3.7 m) long
Order: Testudines
Family: Protostegidae
Range: North America: Kansas, South Dakota
Pn: ar-KEE-lon

Meiolania

This large turtle had large bony spikes on its head. Two of these stuck out on either side, giving the head a width of about 24 inches (60 cm), and would have made it impossible for *Meiolania* to withdraw its head into its shell. The tail was encased in bony armor and ended in a spiked club.

Meiolania

Ple Pleistocene

Size: 8 ft (2.5 m) long
Order: Testudines
Family: Meiolaniidae
Range: Australia
Pn: MY-oh-LAN-ee-ah

Paleotrionyx

Paleotrionyx was a soft-shelled turtle. Its low, rounded shell did not have a covering of horn protecting the bony plates. Instead, a layer of leathery skin covered the shell. It had a long mobile neck and a sharp beak, probably used to crop aquatic weeds and snap up insects and even small fish to eat.

Pa Paleocene

Size: 18 in (45 cm) long
Order: Testudines
Family: Trionychidae
Range: North America
Pn: PAY-lee-oh-TRY-on-ix

Paleotrionyx

Stupendemys

The largest freshwater turtle ever, *Stupendemys* has been extinct for about 3 million years. (The largest freshwater turtle today is only 29 inches (75 cm) long.) This giant lived in water, where it probably fed on weeds, like aquatic turtles today.

Pli Early Pliocene

Size: 6½ ft (2 m) long
Order: Testudines
Family: Pelomedusidae
Range: South America: Venezuela
Pn: styoop-END-em-eez

Stupendemys

Testudo atlas

This was the largest land tortoise ever known and may have weighed as much as 4 tons (4 tonnes). It was more than twice the length of the giant tortoises of today. *Testudo* probably fed on plants. If attacked, it would have pulled its head and legs into its heavy, bony shell for protection.

Ple Pleistocene

Size: 8 ft (2.5 m) long
Order: Testudines
Family: Testudinidae
Range: Asia: India
Pn: TEST-oo-doh-AT-las

Testudo atlas

Lizards and snakes

Today, lizards and snakes are a highly successful group of reptiles, with more than 7,000 species living all over the world except in Antarctica. The first known lizards were small, insect-eating creatures that lived in England during the mid Jurassic. By the Late Jurassic many different types of lizard had developed. Earlier groups of lizardlike reptiles include the sphenodonts, such as *Planocephalosaurus*, and aquatic reptiles such as *Hovasaurus*. Snakes may have evolved from long-bodied, water-living reptiles, such as *Pachyrhachis*.

Megalania

(Ple) Pleistocene

Size: 26 ft (8 m) long
Order: Squamata
Family: Varanidae
Range: Australia
Pn: MEG-ah-LAN-ee-ah

Planocephalosaurus

The sphenodont group, to which this lizardlike creature belonged, first appeared in the Late Triassic. Today the only remaining sphenodont is the tuatara, found in New Zealand. A "living fossil," the tuatara has remained unchanged for 220 million years.

(T) Late Triassic

Size: 8 in (20 cm) long
Order: Sphenodontida
Family: Sphenodontidae
Range: Europe: England
Pn: PLAN-oh-KEF-al-oh-SAW-rus

Planocephalosaurus

Ardeosaurus

Ardeosaurus

An early type of gecko, *Ardeosaurus* had the flattened head and large eyes typical of its modern relatives. Like them, it may have hunted insects and spiders at night, snapping them up in powerful jaws. With its slender body, long tail, and legs sprawled out sideways, *Ardeosaurus* looked very like the lizards of today.

(J) Late Jurassic

Size: 5½ in (14 cm) long
Order: Squamata
Family: Ardeosauridae
Range: Europe: Germany
Pn: AR-dee-oh-SAW-rus

Plotosaurus

Mosasaurs such as *Plotosaurus* were sea-living lizards. The limbs were adapted into short flippers and at the end of the long tail was a vertical fin. The fin would have helped this marine lizard move its large body through the water.

Plotosaurus

Megalania

Monitor lizards first appeared in the Late Cretaceous and have changed little since. *Megalania* may have weighed four times as much as the Komodo dragon—the largest lizard alive today. It probably hunted large marsupials on the plains of Australia where it lived.

Hovasaurus

This lizardlike, aquatic reptile had a tail that was twice the length of its body. The tail, which was deep and flattened from side to side, made an excellent paddle. *Hovasaurus* probably swallowed stones to help it sink in the water when diving for prey.

P Late Permian

Size: 20 in (50 cm) long
Order: Lepidosauromorpha
Family: Tangasauridae
Range: Africa: Madagascar
Pn: HOVE-a-SAW-rus

Hovasaurus

Pleurosaurus

J Late Jurassic

Size: 24 in (60 cm) long
Order: Sphenodontida
Family: Pleurosauridae
Range: Europe: Germany
Pn: PLOO-roh-SAW-rus

Pleurosaurus

Pleurosaurus belonged to a group of slender, snakelike sphenodonts which lived in water. The limbs were tiny, probably of little use on land, and the long tail could have been used to move the reptile through water. Pleurosaurs had extremely long bodies and some species had as many as 57 vertebrae.

Cr Early Cretaceous

Size: 3¼ ft (1 m) long
Order: Squamata
Family: Pachyrhachidae
Range: Asia: Israel
Pn: PAK-ee-RAK-iss

Pachyrhachis

A water-living lizard, *Pachyrhachis* had the long body of a snake and the large head of a monitor lizard. It had tiny back legs and swam by snakelike movements of its long body. This reptile may be one of the ancestors of today's snakes.

Cr Late Cretaceous

Size: 33 ft (10 m) long
Order: Squamata
Family: Mosasauridae
Range: North America: Kansas
Pn: PLOT-oh-SAW-rus

Pachyrhachis

23

Placodonts and nothosaurs

During the time of the dinosaurs, there were several groups of marine reptiles. Least well adapted to marine life were the placodonts of the Triassic. These semiaquatic reptiles were equally at home on the shore or in shallow water, searching for shellfish to eat. Nothosaurs were better suited to life in the sea. They were fish eaters and typically had a streamlined body, long tail, and webbed feet. Both placodonts and nothosaurs died out at the end of the Triassic. Claudiosaurs were an earlier group of semiaquatic reptiles that lived in the Late Permian. They may have been a link between land-living reptiles and later marine reptiles such as nothosaurs and plesiosaurs.

T Triassic

Size: 13 ft (4 m) long
Order: Nothosauria
Family: Nothosauridae
Range: Europe
Pn: seh-REEZ-ee-oh-SAW-rus

Ceresiosaurus

This nothosaur swam by moving its long body and tail from side to side. Like the plesiosaurs of the Jurassic, it used two pairs of paddlelike flippers rather than limbs to help move itself through water. The front flippers were larger than the back flippers and may have provided most of the steering and braking power.

Pistosaurus

Pistosaurus

This marine reptile had features of both the nothosaurs and the plesiosaurs (see pages 26–27). Its body is similar to that of other nothosaurs, but it had a stiff backbone like the plesiosaurs. This meant that it used its paddlelike limbs to push itself through water rather than moving its body and tail.

T Triassic

Size: 10 ft (3 m) long
Order: Nothosauria
Family: Pistosauridae
Range: Europe: France, Germany
Pn: PISS-toe-SAW-rus

Nothosaurus

This typical nothosaur probably lived much as seals do today—fishing at sea and resting on land. Its body and tail were long and flexible and the long toes on each foot were probably webbed for swimming. Its long, slim jaws were lined with sharp teeth—ideal for catching fish.

Nothosaurus

T Triassic

Size: 10 ft (3 m) long
Order: Nothosauria
Family: Nothosauridae
Range: Asia: China, Israel, Russia; Europe; North Africa
Pn: NOTHE-oh-SAW-rus

Ceresiosaurus

T Middle Triassic

Size: 24 in (60 cm) long
Order: Nothosauria
Family: Nothosauridae
Range: Europe: Spain
Pn: LAH-ree-oh-SAW-rus

Lariosaurus

One of the smaller nothosaurs, *Lariosaurus* probably spent much of its time walking on the shore and paddling in shallow coastal water, feeding on small fish and shrimp. It had a shorter neck than most nothosaurs and small toes that would not have been much use for swimming.

Lariosaurus

T Late Triassic

Size: 3¼ ft (1 m) long
Order: Placodontia
Family: Henodontidae
Range: Europe: Germany
Pn: HEN-oh-dus

Claudiosaurus

This lizardlike creature probably lived much like modern marine iguanas. Like them, it may have spent a good deal of its time resting on rocky beaches, warming its body before going hunting. In water, it held its legs against its body to give a more streamlined shape as it searched for food among seaweeds and rocks.

P Late Permian

Size: 24 in (60 cm) long
Order: Lepidosauromorpha
Family: Claudiosauridae
Range: Africa: Madagascar
Pn: CLAWED-ee-oh-SAW-rus

Henodus

Henodus

This placodont had a square-shaped body, covered with bony plates. These made a strong shell to protect it from attack by other marine reptiles such as ichthyosaurs. Although toothless, *Henodus* probably had a horn-covered beak like that of a turtle, which it could use to crush prey such as shellfish.

Claudiosaurus

T Early to Middle Triassic

Size: 6½ ft (2 m) long
Order: Placodontia
Family: Placodontidae
Range: Europe: Alps
Pn: PLAK-oh-dus

Placodus

Placodus had a stocky body and its only aquatic features were its webbed feet and long tail. Its teeth suggest that it fed mostly on shellfish. *Placodus* could have plucked shellfish from the rocks with the blunt teeth sticking out at the front of its jaws and then crushed them with the broad, flat back teeth.

Placodus

Plesiosaurs and ichthyosaurs

Plesiosaurs and ichthyosaurs were the most successful of all the marine reptiles. They dominated the world's seas throughout the Jurassic and Cretaceous periods. There were two groups of plesiosaurs—pliosaurs and the plesiosaurs themselves. Plesiosaurs had long necks and short heads and fed on smaller sea creatures. Pliosaurs were fierce hunters. With their powerful jaws, they could catch sharks and large squid. The ichthyosaurs were best adapted of all to marine life. Typically, they had a streamlined, fishlike body and a tail that could beat from side to side to power their high-speed swimming.

Ophthalmosaurus

J Late Jurassic

Size: 11½ ft (3.5 m) long
Order: Ichthyosauria
Family: Ichthyosauridae
Range: Europe: England, France; western North America; South America: Argentina
Pn: OFF-thal-moh-SAW-rus

Ophthalmosaurus

This ichthyosaur had huge eyes, measuring up to 4 inches (10 cm) across. A ring of bony plates surrounded each eyeball to keep the soft eye from collapsing under the pressure of the water. The large eyes of the *Ophthalmosaurus* suggest that it probably hunted at night.

Elasmosaurus

Elasmosaurus was the longest known plesiosaur. Its neck measured 26 feet (8 m)—more than half of its total length—and contained as many as 71 vertebrae. Its head was relatively small and its jaws were lined with sharply pointed teeth. It probably fed on fish, plunging its long neck into the water to seize its prey.

Elasmosaurus

Cr Late Cretaceous

Size: 46 ft (14 m) long
Order: Plesiosauria
Family: Elasmosauridae
Range: Asia: Japan; North America: Kansas
Pn: eh-LAZ-mo-SAW-rus

Shonisaurus

Liopleurodon

A heavily built pliosaur, *Liopleurodon* had a large head, short, thick neck and a streamlined body. It had big, powerful flippers and would have been able to swim long distances as it chased fast-moving prey such as squid and even other plesiosaurs and ichthyosaurs.

Plesiosaurus

Liopleurodon

J Late Jurassic

Size: 39 ft (12 m) long
Order: Plesiosauria
Family: Pliosauridae
Range: Asia: Russia; Europe: England, France, Germany
Pn: LY-oh-PLOO-ro-don

J Early Jurassic

Size: 7½ ft (2.3 m) long
Order: Plesiosauria
Family: Plesiosauridae
Range: Europe: England, Germany
Pn: PLEEZ-ee-oh-SAW-rus

Plesiosaurus

A typical plesiosaur, with its long neck and small head, *Plesiosaurus* fed on small squid and fish. Its long neck meant that it could have raised its head high above the surface of the sea to search for signs of prey. If it spotted something, it could make a swift lunge to seize the animal in its mouth.

J Early Jurassic Cr Early Cretaceous

Size: 6½ ft (2 m) long
Order: Ichthyosauria
Family: Ichthyosauridae
Range: Europe: England, Germany; Greenland; North America: Alberta
Pn: IK-thee-oh-SAW-rus

Ichthyosaurus

Ichthyosaurus

So many fossils of *Ichthyosaurus* have been found that it is one of the best known of all prehistoric animals. In some of these fossils, the tiny bones of young were inside the adult bodies, showing that ichthyosaurs, like dolphins today, gave birth to live young at sea.

Kronosaurus

T Late Triassic

Size: 49 ft (15 m) long
Order: Ichthyosauria
Family: Shastasauridae
Range: North America: Nevada
Pn: SHOWN-ih-SAW-rus

Shonisaurus

The biggest of the ichthyosaurs, *Shonisaurus* had extremely long jaws, with teeth only at the front. All of its paddlelike flippers were about the same length—in most ichthyosaurs the front flippers were longer than the back pair.

Kronosaurus

The largest-known pliosaur, *Kronosaurus* had a huge, flat-topped skull, measuring almost a quarter of its total body length. A fierce predator, it moved at high speed, flapping its strong flippers up and down as though flying through the water.

Cr Early Cretaceous

Size: 42 ft (12.8 m) long
Order: Plesiosauria
Family: Pliosauridae
Range: Australia: Queensland
Pn: KRONE-oh-SAW-rus

Sea creatures

In the time of the dinosaurs the seas were packed with life. Fish such as *Lepidotes*, their bodies protected by thick bony scales, hunted worms, mollusks, and other small creatures. Crinoids, animals related to starfish, lived on the seabed, catching tiny prey in their feathery, many-branched arms. Also common were belemnites and ammonites, extinct relatives of octopus and squid. Ammonites had a soft body coiled inside a shell with many chambers, whereas belemnites had a straight body and long tentacles, similar to today's squid. Among the biggest creatures were the many types of marine reptiles, such as ichthyosaurs and plesiosaurs, which cruised the oceans preying on fish, squid, and belemnites.

Underwater birth

Ichthyosaurs are thought to have given birth underwater. The young came out tail first, like those of dolphins and whales. This fossil shows a female ichthyosaur with her young just emerging from her body.

In this **Jurassic ocean** a school of belemnites scatters as an *Ichthyosaurus* swims into them, grasping prey in its long jaws. Meanwhile another ichthyosaur, *Eurhinosaurus*, rises to the surface to take a breath.

Ammonite

Plesiosaurus

Lepidotes

Long slender snout

SKELETON OF AN ICHTHYOSAUR

Broad flat snout

Dimorphodon

Paddlelike front limb

Bones supporting tail

SKELETON OF A PLESIOSAUR

Flipper

Marine reptiles

A typical ichthyosaur had a streamlined body, similar to that of a dolphin today. The main swimming power was provided by the large tail, which beat to and fro as the reptile sped through the water. The paddlelike front limbs were used for steering. A plesiosaur swam more slowly, beating its large flippers to move itself along. In contrast to an ichthyosaur, a plesiosaur had a short tail, long neck and relatively small head.

Eurhinosaurus

Ichthyosaurus

Belemnite

29

Crinoid

Early ruling reptiles

Archosaurs, or ruling reptiles, were the group to which dinosaurs belonged. There were several different groups of archosaurs, but the only ones that survive today are the crocodiles. Among the earliest were the proterosuchids, some of which were hunters that resembled crocodiles. Others lived on land. Later came the crurotarsans, such as *Ornithosuchus*, and the aquatic phytosaurs. Aetosaurs, such as *Desmatosuchus*, were the first plant-eating archosaurs and they spread throughout much of the world.

Rutiodon

(T) Middle Triassic

Size: 10 ft (3 m) long
Order: Crurotarsi
Family: Phytosauridae
Range: Europe: Germany, Switzerland; North America
Pn: ROOT-ee-oh-don

Rutiodon

Phytosaurs, such as *Rutiodon*, lived in rivers and lakes, where they fed on fish and other creatures. The body was heavily armored with plates of bone. The long jaws were filled with sharp teeth. Phytosaurs looked very similar to modern crocodiles, but their nostrils were positioned on a bony bump near the eyes, not at the end of the snout as in crocodiles.

(T) Early Triassic

Size: 6½ ft (2 m) long
Order: Archosauria
Family: Proterosuchidae
Range: Asia: China
Pn: PROH-ter-oh-SOO-kus

Proterosuchus

An early proterosuchid, this reptile looked much like a modern crocodile and probably lived in much the same way. It had a slender body and short legs, which sprawled out at the sides of the body. It may have hunted mammal-like reptiles on land as well as fish in water.

Proterosuchus

Erythrosuchus

This early archosaur was one of the biggest land predators of its time. It had a large head and strong jaws lined with sharp teeth. Its legs were held more directly under the body than those of the sprawling *Proterosuchus*, allowing it to move well on land.

(T) Early Triassic

Size: 15 ft (4.5 m) long
Order: Archosauria
Family: Erythrosuchidae
Range: Africa: South Africa
Pn: er-ITH-ro-SOOK-us

Desmatosuchus

Despite its fierce appearance, *Desmatosuchus* was a plant eater with small, leaf-shaped teeth. The bulky body was encased in heavy plates of bone; and a pair of spines, up to 18 inches (45 cm) long, projected sideways from its shoulders. The body armor defended bulky, slow-moving *Desmatosuchus* from predators.

Marasuchus

This reptile shared many skeletal features with dinosaurs, such as front legs that were less than half the length of the back legs. Lightly built and probably a fast mover, it could have run upright on its two back legs as well as on all fours. *Marasuchus* would have fed on smaller reptiles as well as insects.

 Middle
Triassic

Size: 4¼ ft (1.3 m) long
Order: Ornithodira
Family: Lagosuchidae
Range: South America: Argentina
Pn: MAH-rah-SOOK-us

Marasuchus

Ornithosuchus

Ornithosuchus looked remarkably like a dinosaur. Its back legs were held vertically beneath its body and it could probably move upright on two legs. The structure of its ankle joints, however, was different from that of true dinosaurs.

Ornithosuchus

T Late
Triassic

Size: 10 ft (3 m) long
Order: Crurotarsi
Family: Ornithosuchidae
Range: Europe: Scotland
Pn: OR-nith-oh-SOOK-us

T Early
Triassic

Size: 20 in (50 cm) long
Order: Archosauria
Family: Euparkeriidae
Range: Africa: South Africa
Pn: YOO-park-EE-ree-a

T Late
Triassic

Size: 16 ft (5 m) long
Order: Crurotarsi
Family: Stagonolepididae
Range: North America: Texas
Pn: DEZ-mat-oh-SOOK-us

Euparkeria

Euparkeria

This little archosaur was a slimly built creature with a light armor of bony plates running down its back and tail. It could probably rear up on its back legs to run away from danger and its long tail would have helped balance its body as it ran. A carnivore, it had long sharp teeth.

Desmatosuchus

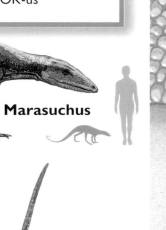

31

Crocodiles

The first crocodiles appeared in the Triassic, some 220 million years ago, and are the only members of the archosaur, or ruling reptile group (see pages 30–31), alive today. The earliest examples of the order Crocodylia, such as *Terrestrisuchus*, were lightly built long-legged creatures, which probably fed on insects. True crocodiles evolved in the Jurassic and look remarkably similar to modern crocodiles. Some lived on land, whereas others were semiaquatic as crocodiles are today. A few families, such as the metriorhynchs, were adapted to life in the sea. All crocodiles, even the early ones, have long narrow skulls with muscles set far back to allow the jaws to open wide for grasping large prey.

J Middle to Late Jurassic

Size: 10 ft (3 m) long
Order: Crocodylia
Family: Metriorhynchidae
Range: Europe: England, France; South America: Chile
Pn: MET-ree-oh-RINK-us

Metriorhynchus

This crocodile and other members of its family were well adapted for life in the sea. Its limbs were paddlelike flippers and its tail had a large fishlike fin for swimming. It did not have bony protective plates on its body like crocodiles today—these would have made its body too heavy in the water.

Protosuchus

J Early Jurassic

Size: 3 ft (90 cm) long
Order: Crocodylia
Family: Protosuchidae
Range: North America: Arizona
Pn: PROE-toh-SOOK-us

Deinosuchus

Only a skull, measuring more than 6½ feet (2 m), has been found of *Deinosuchus*, showing that it was probably the biggest crocodile of all time. It may have lived much like the crocodiles of today, but some scientists believe that *Deinosuchus* had longer legs than modern crocodiles and lived on land, preying on dinosaurs.

Protosuchus

Fossils of *Protosuchus* have been found in the same rocks as the remains of dinosaurs. This suggests that this land-living crocodile preyed on other land creatures. Like today's crocodiles, *Protosuchus* had a pair of long teeth at the front of the lower jaw that fitted into notches on the upper jaw when the mouth was closed.

Cr Late Cretaceous

Size: 49 ft (15 m) long
Order: Crocodylia
Family: Alligatoridae
Range: North America: Texas
Pn: DINE-oh-SOOK-us

Metriorhynchus

Terrestrisuchus

An early member of the crocodile group, this lightly built reptile had long back legs and may have moved upright. It probably fed on insects and other small creatures. Although *Terrestrisuchus* does not look like a crocodile, there are many typical features of the group in the bone structure of its skull and front limbs.

T Late Triassic

Size: 20 in (50 cm) long
Order: Crocodylia
Family: Saltoposuchidae
Range: Europe: Wales
Pn: ter-EST-ri-SOOK-us

Terrestrisuchus

Bernissartia

This little crocodile probably lived in water and on land. It had two types of teeth in its jaws. At the front were long, pointed teeth, suitable for catching fish. At the back were broader, flatter teeth, which could have been used to crush shellfish or the bones of dead animals.

Bernissartia

Deinosuchus

Cr Early Cretaceous

Size: 24 in (60 cm) long
Order: Crocodylia
Family: Bernissartiidae
Range: Europe: Belgium, England
Pn: BER-nih-SART-ee-ah

Teleosaurus

A sea-living crocodile, *Teleosaurus* had extremely long, narrow jaws lined with many sharp teeth. These teeth interlocked when the mouth was closed, forming a trap ideal for catching slippery fish or squid. It probably swam by moving its long slender body and tail, with its short front legs held against its body.

Teleosaurus

J Early Jurassic

Size: 10 ft (3 m) long
Order: Crocodylia
Family: Teleosauridae
Range: Europe: France
Pn: TELL-ee-oh-SAW-rus

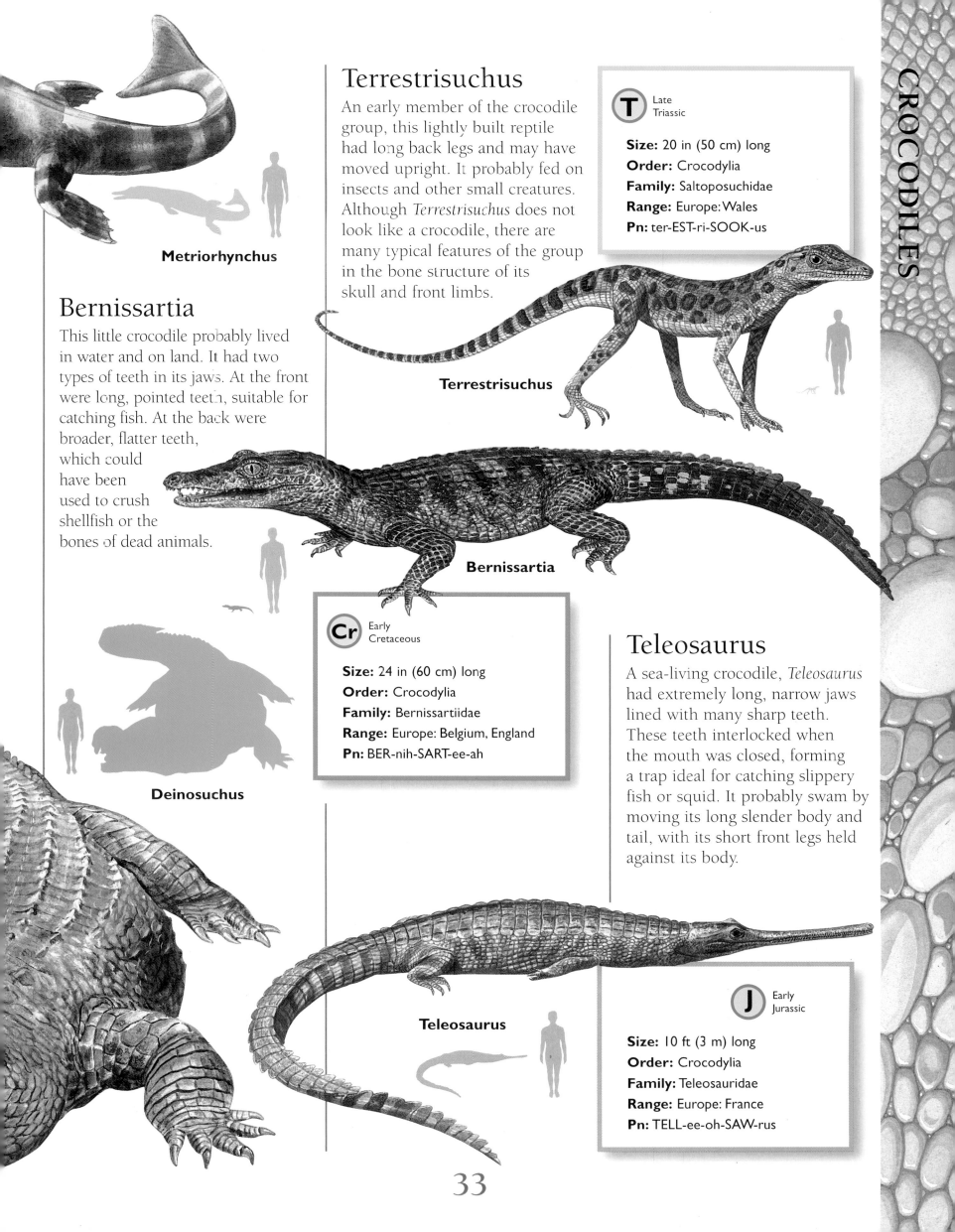

33

Flying reptiles

Pterosaurs were the first vertebrates (animals with backbones) to take to life in the air. They first evolved in the Late Triassic and became extinct at the end of the Cretaceous at the same time as the dinosaurs. More than 120 different species of pterosaur have been discovered so far. All had wings that were attached to an extremely long fourth finger on each hand and to the sides of the pterosaur's body. The earliest pterosaurs were the rhamphorhynchoids, which had a long tail and short neck. Later came the pterodactyloids, which grew much larger and typically had a short tail and long neck and skull.

J Late Jurassic

Size: 3¼ ft (1 m) wingspan
Order: Pterosauria
Family: Rhamphorhynchidae
Range: Europe: Germany; Africa: Tanzania
Pn: RAM-for-INK-us

Rhamphorhynchus

Eudimorphodon

Eudimorphodon

T Late Triassic

Size: 29 in (75 cm) wingspan
Order: Pterosauria
Family: Dimorphodontidae
Range: Europe: Italy
Pn: yoo-dee-MORF-oh-don

Eudimorphodon

This rhamphorhynchoid is one of the earliest pterosaurs known. It had a long bony tail, which made up about half its total length. Like many other pterosaurs, it had a small diamond-shaped flap at the tip of the tail that may have acted like a rudder to help the pterosaur change direction in the air.

J Late Jurassic

Size: 3¼ ft (1 m) wingspan
Order: Pterosauria
Family: Rhamphorhynchidae
Range: Europe: England
Pn: SKAF-og-NAY-thus

Scaphognathus

Studies of the brain cavity of one fossil of this pterosaur have shown that its brain was much larger than that of other reptiles of a similar size. The relative sizes of different areas of the brain suggest that this pterosaur, and probably its relatives, had excellent eyesight but a poor sense of smell.

Quetzalcoatlus

Although known only from a few wing bones, this pterodactyloid is thought to have been the biggest flying animal ever. Its remains were found in an area of Texas that was once marshland. Like a giant egret, *Quetzalcoatlus* may have waded through the marsh, snatching fish with its long jaws.

Scaphognathus

34

Rhamphorhynchus

Well-preserved fossils of this pterosaur found in the limestone of Solnhofen in Germany reveal even the fine structure of its wings. These show that thin fibers ran from the front to the back of the wings, giving them extra strength. This pterosaur had long jaws filled with sharp teeth and probably fed on fish.

Dimorphodon

This pterosaur had an unusually large head, similar in shape to a puffin's. Inside the mouth were two types of teeth—spiky ones at the front and much smaller teeth farther back. These may have helped the pterosaur to catch insects in the air or on the ground.

J Early Jurassic

Size: 29 in (75 cm) wingspan
Order: Pterosauria
Family: Dimorphodontidae
Range: Europe: England
Pn: dy-MORF-oh-don

Dimorphodon

Pterodactylus

Like many pterosaurs, *Pterodactylus* probably fed on fish. Its long narrow jaws, lined with sharp teeth, would have been ideal for grasping and holding its slippery prey. With its short tail and long neck, it was a typical pterodactyloid.

Pterodaustro

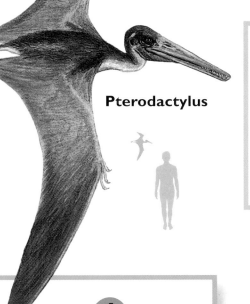

Pterodactylus

Quetzalcoatlus

J Late Jurassic

Size: 4 ft (1.2 m) wingspan
Order: Pterosauria
Family: Pterodaustridae
Range: South America: Argentina
Pn: TER-oh-DOW-stro

Cr Late Cretaceous

Size: 39 ft (12 m) wingspan
Order: Pterosauria
Family: Azhdarchidae
Range: North America: Texas
Pn: KWET-zal-KO-at-lus

J Late Jurassic

Size: 29 in (75 cm) wingspan
Order: Pterosauria
Family: Pterodactylidae
Range: Europe: England, France, Germany; Africa: Tanzania
Pn: TER-oh-DAK-ty-lus

Pterodaustro

Pterodaustro had long jaws, which curved upward at the tips. The lower jaw was packed with fine teeth and there were also tiny teeth in the upper jaw. It may have fed by skimming along the surface of the sea. As water flowed through its open mouth, tiny creatures would have been caught on the sievelike teeth.

Flying reptiles

Pterosaurs lived at the same time as dinosaurs and may share the same ancestor. Scientists now believe that these flying reptiles were good, if slow, fliers, able to flap their wings as birds do, rather than just gliding through the air. They may not have been able to take off from the ground but could have launched themselves into the air from a perch in a tree or on a rock. Pterosaurs ate a range of foods. Those with long skulls and sharp teeth probably fed on fish. Others may have caught insects or even fed on plants. The long beak of *Tapejara*, for example, may have been used to pick fruit.

This pterosaur, named **Pterodactylus,** lived in Europe in Jurassic times. The well-preserved fossil clearly shows the body structure, including the slender jaws and the extra-long fingers that supported the wings.

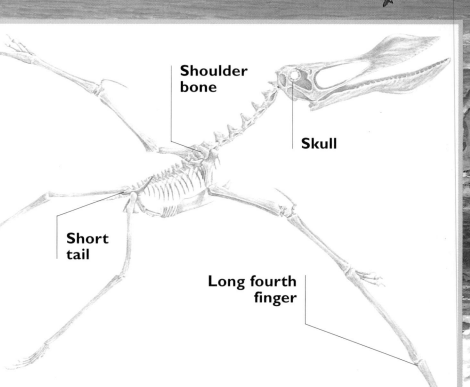

Cearadactylus

Shoulder bone

Skull

Short tail

Long fourth finger

Pterosaur skeleton

A pterosaur had an extremely light skeleton so that it was able to fly. Its bones were slender and many were also hollow to make them lighter still. Its first three fingers were short and tipped with sharp claws, but the fourth finger was very long and helped to support the wing. The wing was also attached to the side of the body. On each foot were five toes. Four were long and tipped with claws. The fifth toe was short and did not have a claw.

Santanadactylus

Cretaceous pterosaurs

In this scene of 100 million years ago, pterosaurs soar over the ocean, searching for fish to catch. *Tapejara*, a pterosaur with a huge prow on its upper jaw, heads inland. On the rocks *Tropeognathus* moves around on all fours, using the claws on its wings as well as its feet.

Tropeognathus

Tapejara

A Late Cretaceous pterosaur, *Anhanguera* probably fed on fish, swooping down to the surface of the sea to grasp its prey and carrying it off to eat. Its long slender jaws and sharp teeth were ideally shaped for holding slippery fish.

37

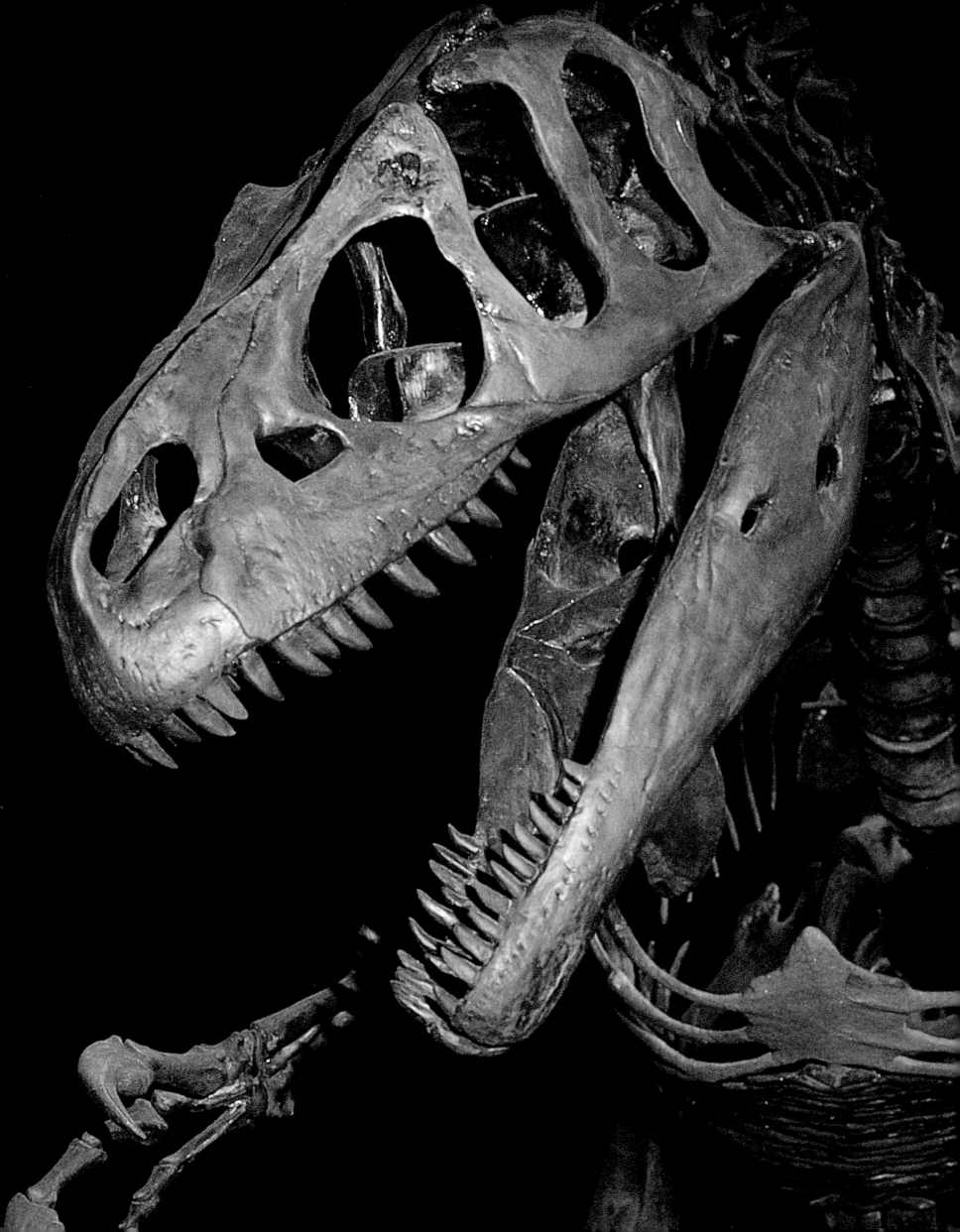

Dinosaurs

These amazing reptiles were probably the most successful animals that have ever lived. The first dinosaurs lived about 225 million years ago, during the Triassic period, and more and more species developed during the Jurassic and Cretaceous periods. Dinosaurs became large and widespread until they mysteriously disappeared at the end of the Cretaceous about 65 million years ago.

Dinosaurs were living, breathing creatures that had to find food, defend themselves against enemies, and look after their young—just as animals do today. Although no human has ever seen a living dinosaur, we know something of how they looked and the way they behaved from the fossils and other remains that have been discovered. Bones show the shape and size of dinosaurs, teeth provide clues about what they ate, while fossil tracks can give an idea of how fast they moved.

With its huge, daggerlike teeth and powerful jaws, **Allosaurus** would have been a fearsome sight as it preyed on plant-eating dinosaurs. It lived in Jurassic times and its fossilized remains have been found in western North America.

Corythosaurus

39

What was a dinosaur?

A dinosaur was a type of reptile and had a bony skeleton and thick leathery skin. More than 500 species of dinosaurs have been discovered so far and there may be many more yet to be found. They ranged in size from creatures of 3¼ feet (1 m) long to giants of 100 feet (30 m) or more. Dinosaurs all lived on land and are believed to have laid eggs. There were two groups of dinosaurs, saurischians and ornithischians, which differed in the structure of their hip bones. All ornithischians fed on plants, but the saurischian group included fierce, meat-eating hunters as well as plant eaters.

A **dramatic encounter** between the meat-eating tyrannosaur *Albertosaurus* and the plant-eating horned dinosaur *Centrosaurus* is reconstructed in this display at the Royal Tyrrell Museum in Drumheller, Canada.

Lizard

Ways of moving

Most early reptiles moved like lizards today, with their legs sprawled out to the sides. Dinosaurs had a much better way of moving. Their legs were held straight down beneath the body, which meant they could carry more weight and take longer, faster strides.

Dinosaur

40

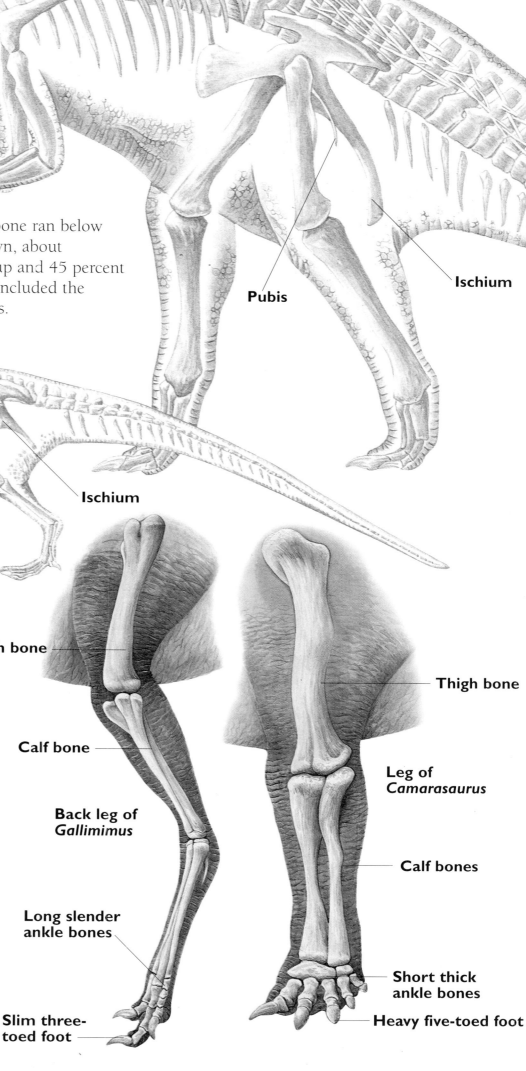

A skeleton of the ornithischian dinosaur *Iguanodon*

The two groups of dinosaurs

Saurischian dinosaurs, such as *Ornitholestes*, had a pubis bone that pointed away from the ischium bone. In ornithischian dinosaurs, such as *Iguanodon*, the pubis bone ran below the ischium bone. Of the dinosaurs known, about 55 percent belong to the saurischian group and 45 percent to the ornithischian group. Saurischians included the sauropods, the biggest of all dinosaurs.

Pubis

Ischium

Ischium

Pubis

A skeleton of the saurischian dinosaur *Ornitholestes*

Dinosaur legs

Slender, birdlike dinosaurs, such as *Gallimimus*, had long thigh and calf bones with big muscles in the thigh to power the leg. The ankle and foot bones were also long and slim. Such dinosaurs could probably run at up to 40 mph (65 km/h). The legs of sauropods such as *Camarasaurus* were very different. The bones were large and bulky and the foot spread out to form a large pad to support the dinosaur's massive weight. Sauropods plodded along on all four legs, whereas *Gallimimus* ran on its two slender back legs.

Thigh bone

Thigh bone

Calf bone

Leg of *Camarasaurus*

Back leg of *Gallimimus*

Calf bones

Long slender ankle bones

Short thick ankle bones

Slim three-toed foot

Heavy five-toed foot

A dinosaur family tree

The word "dinosaur," meaning "terrible lizard," was first used in 1842 by Richard Owen, one of the first experts on these reptiles. Since then, views on the relationships between the different groups of dinosaurs have changed dramatically as more species are found and new discoveries made. The chart here shows a dinosaur family tree that is accepted by most experts and includes all known types of dinosaurs. It also shows the close relationship of birds (Aves) to dinosaurs.

SAUROPODOMORPHA

THEROPODA

SAURISCHIA

DINOSAURIA

ORNITHISCHIA

Dinosaur groups

All dinosaurs fall into one of two groups, or orders—Saurischia and Ornithischia. These in turn are subdivided into smaller groups right down to family level—a family is a group of dinosaur species with shared characteristics. Family names end in "idae." Where there is only one type, or genus, in a family the genus name is given instead of a family name and it is shown in *italics*. A broken line is shown for *Eoraptor,* which may be the earliest of all dinosaurs.

GENASAURIA

THYREOPHORA

CERAPODA

ORNITHOPODA

Nineteenth-century British paleontologist **Richard Owen** worked on a number of life-sized models of dinosaurs for an exhibition in London. In 1853, a special dinner held in his honor took place in the half-completed model of an *Iguanodon.*

Eoraptor
Herrerasauridae
Ceratosauria
Abelisauridae
Podokesauridae
Megalosauridae
Compsognathus
Coelurus
Allosauridae
Spinosauridae
Dromaeosauridae
Other birds
Archaeopteryx
Oviraptoridae
Therizinosauridae
Tyrannosauridae
Troodontidae
Ornithomimidae
Thecodontosauridae
Plateosauridae
Melanorosauridae
Anchisauridae
Vulcanodontidae
Barapasaurus
Euhelopodidae
Cetiosauridae
Brachiosauridae
Camarasauridae
Titanosauridae
Nemegtosauridae
Diplodocidae
Pisanosaurus
Fabrosauridae
Scelidosauridae
Ankylosauridae
Nodosauridae
Stegosauria
Pachycephalosauridae
Homalocephalidae
Protoceratopsidae
Ceratopsidae
Psittacosauridae
Heterodontosauridae
Hypsilophodontidae
Iguanodontidae
Ouranosaurus
Hadrosauridae

AVES
MANIRAPTORA
TETANURAE
COELUROSAURIA
PACHYCEPHALOSAURIA
CERATOPSIA

Ceratosaurs

Ceratosaurs were meat-eating dinosaurs, ranging from tiny *Compsognathus* to large predators such as *Carnotaurus*. The group includes about 20 dinosaurs, the earliest known being *Coelophysis*, which dates from the Late Triassic. All walked upright on their back legs and had short arms. Several ceratosaurs had strangely shaped crests or horns on their heads. These were probably not used in battle but in visual displays for attracting mates in the breeding season.

Herrerasaurus

T Late Triassic

Size: 10 ft (3 m) long
Order: Saurischia
Family: Herrerasauridae
Range: South America: Argentina
Pn: eh-ray-rah-SORE-us

Eoraptor

Ceratosaurus

With its powerful jaws armed with sharp, curved teeth, *Ceratosaurus* would have been a fierce hunter. On its short arms were hands with four strong clawed fingers and the long legs had three clawed toes on each foot. A row of bony plates ran down the center of the back and tail, and on its snout was a small horn. The horn seems to be too small to have been used for defense and may have been only for display.

Herrerasaurus

One of the earliest known dinosaurs, *Herrerasaurus* had a slender body and a long narrow head. It would have moved upright on its legs, which were more than twice the length of its arms. Its fingers were strong and had large curved claws for grasping prey. Sliding joints in the lower jaws allowed more flexibility when biting.

T Late Triassic

Size: 3¼ ft (1 m) long
Order: Theropoda
Family: Eoraptoridae
Range: South America: Argentina
Pn: ee-oh-RAP-tor

Eoraptor

Like *Herrerasaurus*, *Eoraptor* was one of the earliest known dinosaurs. It was also a carnivore but was smaller and more lightly built than its relative. Its teeth were sharp and slightly serrated for cutting through meat, but it did not have the flexible jaw joint of *Herrerasaurus*.

Ceratosaurus

J Late Jurassic

Size: 20 ft (6 m) long
Order: Saurischia
Family: Ceratosauridae
Range: North America: Colorado, Wyoming
Pn: SER-a-toe-SAW-rus

Compsognathus

One of the smallest of all dinosaurs, *Compsognathus* was probably not much bigger than a chicken. Its body was designed for speed, with lightweight bones, a long tail and long slender legs. Small reptiles were probably its main prey—the remains of a lizard were found in one fossilized skeleton of *Compsognathus*.

Compsognathus

J Early Jurassic

Size: 20 ft (6 m) long
Order: Saurischia
Family: Ceratosauridae
Range: North America: Arizona
Pn: die-LOAF-oh-SAW-rus

J Late Jurassic

Size: 24 in (60 cm) long
Order: Saurischia
Family: Compsognathidae
Range: Europe: Germany, France
Pn: komp-soh-NAY-thus

Dilophosaurus

Coelophysis

Coelophysis

Built for speed, *Coelophysis* had a light slender body and long slim legs and tail. The narrow jaws were lined with sharp serrated teeth for attacking prey. Remains of more than 1,000 skeletons were found in New Mexico, suggesting that this dinosaur lived in herds.

Dilophosaurus

This dinosaur had a pair of semicircular bony crests, one on each side of its skull. Some experts believe that only the males had these crests and that they were used in displays to attract females. Its teeth were sharp but slender, suggesting that this dinosaur may have killed its prey with its clawed feet and hands rather than with its jaws.

T Late Triassic

Size: up to 10 ft (3 m) long
Order: Saurischia
Family: Podokesauridae
Range: North America: Connecticut, New Mexico
Pn: seel-oh-FY-sis

Carnotaurus

Carnotaurus

Discovered in 1985, this dinosaur had a deep, bull-like head with big horns above the eyes—its name means "meat-eating bull." Its arms were extremely small and probably almost useless. Well-preserved skin impressions found near the bones show that small cone-shaped spines covered the sides of its body.

Cr Mid to Late Cretaceous

Size: 24½ ft (7.5 m) long
Order: Saurischia
Family: Abelisauridae
Range: South America: Argentina
Pn: kar-noh-TORE-us

45

Tetanurans

The tetanurans were a group of large predatory dinosaurs that lived in the Jurassic and Cretaceous periods. Despite their appearance, these dinosaurs were closely related to birds. They included groups such as the allosaurs and megalosaurs as well as a number of more recently discovered dinosaurs such as *Giganotosaurus*. All the tetanurans had a large opening in each upper jaw bone that made the skull much lighter than it looks. The rear part of the tail was stiffened by special interlocking bony structures on the vertebrae—the name tetanuran means "stiff tail."

Allosaurus

Allosaurus

Mighty *Allosaurus* probably weighed between 1 and 2 tons (1–2 tonnes) and stood about 15 feet (4.5 m) tall. Packs of these fierce dinosaurs may have hunted together so they could bring down even larger creatures, such as sauropods and stegosaurs.

J Late Jurassic

Size: up to 33 ft (10 m) long
Order: Saurischia
Family: Allosauridae
Range: Asia: China
Pn: yang-choo-AN-oh-SAW-rus

Yangchuanosaurus

Yangchuanosaurus

This dinosaur was first discovered in China in 1978. A typical allosaur, it had a huge head, powerful jaws and jagged-edged teeth. Its long tail made up about half of its body length and helped to balance the heavy body as the dinosaur strode along on its sturdy legs.

Giganotosaurus

Cr Late Cretaceous

Size: 43 ft (13 m) long
Order: Saurischia
Family: Abelisauridae
Range: South America: Patagonia
Pn: jig-a-NOT-o-SAW-rus

Giganotosaurus

First discovered in South America in 1993, *Giganotosaurus* was one of the largest of all meat-eating dinosaurs. It may have weighed as much as 8 tons (7.2 tonnes). As well as hunting its own prey, it may have scared other predators away and stolen their catches.

J Late Jurassic   **Cr** Early Cretaceous

Size: up to 39 ft (12 m) long
Order: Saurischia
Family: Allosauridae
Range: North America: Colorado, Utah, Wyoming; Africa: Tanzania; Australia
Pn: AL-oh-SAW-rus

J Jurassic

Size: 30 ft (9 m) long
Order: Saurischia
Family: Megalosauridae
Range: Europe: England, France; Africa: Morocco
Pn: MEG-ah-loh-SAW-rus

Megalosaurus

Cr Early Cretaceous

Size: 26 ft (8 m) long
Order: Saurischia
Family: uncertain
Range: Africa: Egypt, Morocco, Tunisia
Pn: kar-kar-o-DON-toh-SAW-rus

Megalosaurus

This was the first dinosaur to be scientifically named in England, in 1824. A typical meat eater, it had a large head, powerful jaws and curved, saw-edged teeth. With its strong, clawed fingers and toes, it was well equipped to attack large plant-eating dinosaurs.

Carcharodontosaurus

Carcharodontosaurus

In 1996, scientists discovered fossils of a giant meat-eating dinosaur in the Moroccan desert. Its skull alone measured more than 5 feet (1.5 m) and was longer than that of *Tyrannosaurus*. Its teeth were 5 inches (12 cm) long, giving this dinosaur its name, which means "shark-toothed reptile."

Cryolophosaurus

This large meat eater was discovered in Antarctica in 1994. It had a unique crest which ran across its skull, with two small horns on each side. The crest was too thin to have been a weapon so experts think that it was probably used for display during the mating season.

Cryolophosaurus

Suchomimus

Fossils of this dinosaur were discovered in 1998 in the Sahara Desert. A member of a group of fish-eating dinosaurs called spinosaurs, it had a long narrow snout like a crocodile and thumb claws measuring 12 inches (30 cm).

Cr Early Cretaceous

Size: 33 ft (10 m) long
Order: Saurischia
Family: Spinosauridae
Range: Africa: Niger
Pn: SOOK-o-MEEM-us

J Early Jurassic

Size: 23–26 ft (7–8 m) long
Order: Saurischia
Family: uncertain
Range: Antarctica
Pn: cry-oh-LOAF-oh-SAW-rus

Suchomimus

47

Jurassic times

During the Jurassic period, which began 208 million years ago, the climate became wetter and thick plants, such as ferns, conifers, and ginkgos, covered much of the land. New kinds of dinosaurs developed, feeding on the lush plant life. These included sauropods, which were the biggest creatures ever to live on land; they ate more than 1 ton (1 tonne) of plant food a day. Plentiful prey also allowed more types of meat-eating dinosaur to thrive. In the air were flying insects and pterosaurs, as well as the first species of birds.

Shunosaurus, a sauropod

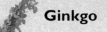

Ginkgo

Tree fern

Frog

The Jurassic world

During the Jurassic period the supercontinent of Pangaea split into two, creating the land areas of Laurasia in the north and Gondwana in the south. The climate was still warm all over the world but rainfall increased.

Siberia

LAURASIA

China

Europe

NORTH America

Turkey Iran

Spain

Tibet

PACIFIC OCEAN

TETHYS OCEAN

EQUATOR

South America Africa

southwest China

GONDWANA

India

Australia

Antarctica

Key to map

Ocean

Landmass

Sea-covered continent

Mid Jurassic China

In this mid-Jurassic scene in what is now southwest China, a stegosaur, *Huayangosaurus*, rears back in fear as fast-moving meat eaters, *Gasosaurus*, approach. Sauropods, *Shunosaurus*, look up from feeding on tree ferns—despite their great bulk even they could fall prey to a group of these sharp-toothed predators.

Angustinaripterus, a flying reptile (pterosaur)

Ginkgo

Conifer

Gasosaurus, a tetanuran

Cycad

Huayangosaurus, a stegosaur

Fern

Salamander

Horsetails

49

Bird relatives

This group, known as the Maniraptora, includes several types of birdlike dinosaur, such as dromaeosaurs and troodontids, as well as birds themselves. A feature shared by all of these creatures was a special flexible wrist joint that allowed the front limb to be folded against the body. The dinosaurs in this group were probably all fast-moving hunters that ran on two legs. *Archaeopteryx*, the earliest known bird, lived about 150 million years ago and had features of both birds and reptiles. Like birds today, it had wings and a covering of feathers. But like reptiles, it had toothed jaws and a long bony tail.

Stenonychosaurus

Compared to its body size, *Stenonychosaurus* had the biggest brain of any dinosaur. It also had large eyes, measuring about 2 inches (5 cm) across. A slender creature, built for fast running, it probably hunted at night.

Cr Late Cretaceous

Size: 6½ ft (2 m) long
Order: Saurischia
Family: Troodontidae
Range: North America: Alberta
Pn: STEN-oh-nike-o-SAW-rus

Velociraptor

Stenonychosaurus

Cr Late Cretaceous

Size: 6 ft (1.8 m) long
Order: Saurischia
Family: Dromaeosauridae
Range: Asia: Mongolia, China
Pn: vel-O-si-RAP-tor

Velociraptor

A fast-moving hunter, *Velociraptor* had a long, flat-snouted head. Two fossilized skeletons found in Mongolia revealed *Velociraptor* locked in battle with a horned dinosaur, *Protoceratops* (see page 87). Scientists think that the two may have died in a sandstorm that developed during the attack.

Archaeopteryx

Archaeopteryx

Unlike birds today, *Archaeopteryx* did not have a large breastbone to support powerful flying muscles. It probably could not fly far and may have had to climb up trees in order to launch itself into the air and then flap and glide short distances in search of insect prey.

J Late Jurassic

Size: 14 in (35 cm) long
Order: Saurischia: Aves
Family: Archaeopterygidae
Range: Europe: Germany
Pn: ark-ee-OP-ter-iks

Deinonychus

A fast, agile predator, *Deinonychus* had a special weapon. The second toe on each foot bore a large curved claw, 5 inches (12 cm) long. The dinosaur could have stood on one leg and used the claw of the other foot to slash into its victim's flesh.

Cr Early Cretaceous

Size: 10–13 ft (3–4 m) long
Order: Saurischia
Family: Dromaeosauridae
Range: North America: Montana
Pn: die-NON-i-kus

Deinonychus

Dromaeosaurus

Like *Deinonychus*, this dinosaur had large, curved claws on its feet that it used as weapons to kill prey. This fierce, fast-moving creature probably hunted in packs that could have brought down animals much larger than themselves.

Saurornithoides

Like *Stenonychosaurus*, this dinosaur had a big brain and probably had well-developed senses. Its eyes were large, suggesting that it may have been active at night, coming out to hunt small reptiles and other creatures.

Cr Late Cretaceous

Size: 6½ ft (2 m) long
Order: Saurischia
Family: Troodontidae
Range: Asia: Mongolia
Pn: sore-OR-nith-oid-eez

Saurornithoides

Scipionyx

This creature was only named as a dinosaur in 1998, although the fossil was discovered 10 years earlier. The fossil is unique in that it contains parts of the gut—the first ever evidence of the internal organs of a dinosaur. *Scipionyx* was probably a meat eater and ran upright on two legs.

Cr Late Cretaceous

Size: 6 ft (1.8 m) long
Order: Saurischia
Family: Dromaeosauridae
Range: North America: Alberta
Pn: DROH-may-oh-SORE-us

Cr Early Cretaceous

Size: 20–39 in (50 cm–1 m) long
Order: Saurischia
Family: uncertain
Range: Europe: Italy
Pn: skip-ee-OH-nix

Dromaeosaurus

Scipionyx

51

Ostrich dinosaurs

With their slender legs, long necks, and small heads, the ostrich dinosaurs looked similar to the ostriches of today. Like ostriches, the ostrich dinosaurs were fast runners and may have been able to sprint along at up to 40 mph (65 km/h) as they searched for food such as lizards and frogs. They may also have eaten leaves and fruit, which they could have pulled from the trees with the slender clawed fingers on their hands. Possible relatives of the ornithomimids are the therizinosaurids (also known as segnosaurids). Complete skeletons of these creatures have only recently been discovered. Unlike other theropods, they probably fed on plants.

Oviraptor

The name of this dinosaur means "egg thief" because the first fossil was found with a clutch of eggs. It was thought that these belonged to another dinosaur and that *Oviraptor* was raiding the nest. Now scientists have discovered that the eggs belonged to *Oviraptor* and it probably died defending its eggs.

Cr Late Cretaceous

Size: 6 ft (1.8 m) long
Order: Saurischia
Family: Oviraptoridae
Range: Asia: Mongolia
Pn: OHV-ih-RAP-tor

Ornithomimus

A typical ostrich dinosaur, *Ornithomimus* had a lightly built body and slender back legs. As it ran, the dinosaur would have held its long tail straight out behind to help balance the weight of its body. It had no teeth but it used its hard beak to chop its food into pieces that it could swallow.

Ornithomimus

Cr Late Cretaceous

Size: 11½ ft (3.5 m) long
Order: Saurischia
Family: Ornithomimidae
Range: North America: Colorado, Montana; Asia: Tibet
Pn: or-NITH-oh-MEEM-us

Dromiceiomimus

Dromiceiomimus

Skulls of this ostrich dinosaur show that it had a huge brain and large eyes—larger than those of any modern land animal. It probably hunted at night, catching small mammals and lizards in its toothless beak. Its legs were particularly long so it was probably a very fast runner.

Cr Late Cretaceous

Size: 11½ ft (3.5 m) long
Order: Saurischia
Family: Ornithomimidae
Range: North America: Alberta
Pn: droh-MEE-see-oh-MEEM-us

Oviraptor

Pelecanimimus

This was the first ostrich dinosaur to be discovered in Europe. It had a long narrow skull and fossil impressions reveal that it may have had a throat pouch like a pelican. Unlike other ostrich dinosaurs, *Pelecanimimus* had a large number of teeth in its long jaws—as many as 220.

Pelecanimimus

Cr Early Cretaceous

Size: up to 6½ ft (2 m) long
Order: Saurischia
Family: Ornithomimidae
Range: Europe: Spain
Pn: pel-e-KAN-i-MEEM-us

Therizinosaurus

The few fossils that have been found so far of *Therizinosaurus* show a creature with arms bearing huge sickle-shaped claws more than 27 inches (70 cm) long. The dinosaur may have used these claws to gather leaves and pass them to its toothless beak.

Therizinosaurus

Cr Late Cretaceous

Size: 13–16 ft (4–5 m) long
Order: Saurischia
Family: Therizinosauridae
Range: Asia: Mongolia, China
Pn: thair-uh-ZEEN-uh-SAW-rus

Alxasaurus

Cr Early Cretaceous

Size: up to 13 ft (4 m) long
Order: Saurischia
Family: Therizinosauridae
Range: Asia: Mongolia, China
Pn: AHL-shah-SAW-rus

Gallimimus

Alxasaurus

A relative of *Therizinosaurus*, *Alxasaurus* also had long slender arms and hands with huge claws. Its body was bulky with large hips and a short tail, which it may have used to help prop itself up as it fed. The small head ended in a toothless beak, but there were some small teeth farther back in the jaws.

Cr Late Cretaceous

Size: 13 ft (4 m) long
Order: Saurischia
Family: Ornithomimidae
Range: Asia: Mongolia
Pn: gal-lee-MEEM-us

Gallimimus

One of the largest of the ostrich dinosaurs, *Gallimimus* was twice the size of a modern ostrich. Like the rest of its group, it did not have strong teeth or sharp claws to defend itself from attackers. Instead it relied on speed—few other dinosaurs could catch it when it ran.

53

Tyrannosaurs

Huge, flesh-eating dinosaurs, tyrannosaurs lived in Asia and North America during the Late Cretaceous. They were among the largest land carnivores that have ever lived. All tyrannosaurs had massive heads and strong jaws lined with sharp teeth, some of which were up to 6 inches (15 cm) long. They walked upright on their two back legs and could probably move at 20 mph (30 km/h) or more. Their front limbs were so small they did not even reach the mouth. Some experts think that a tyrannosaur may have used its tiny arms to lift itself off the ground after sleeping or feeding.

Daspletosaurus

Cr Late Cretaceous

Size: 28 ft (8.5 m) long
Order: Saurischia
Family: Tyrannosauridae
Range: North America: Alberta
Pn: das-PLEE-toh-SAW-rus

Daspletosaurus

Although this dinosaur was smaller than *Tyrannosaurus*, it was still a fierce hunter. Equipped with large, saw-edged teeth, clawed feet and a powerful body, *Daspletosaurus* could have hunted the large horned dinosaurs that lived in the North American forests at the time.

Siamotyrannus

First discovered in Thailand in 1996, this creature may be the oldest known tyrannosaur. It lived some 50 million years before *Tyrannosaurus*. Like its relative, *Siamotyrannus* had jagged, curved teeth and probably fed on plant-eating dinosaurs much larger than itself.

Siamotyrannus

Cr Early Cretaceous

Size: 16–23 ft (5–7 m) long
Order: Saurischia
Family: Tyrannosauridae
Range: Asia: Thailand
Pn: sigh-AM-oh-TIE-ran-us

Alioramus

While most tyrannosaurs had deep skulls and short snouts, *Alioramus* had a long narrow skull. There were also a number of bony knobs on the snout and near the eyes. Like other tyrannosaurs, it may have lain in wait for prey, ready to pounce when the victim came near.

Alioramus

Cr Late Cretaceous

Size: 20 ft (6 m) long
Order: Saurischia
Family: Tyrannosauridae
Range: Asia: Mongolia
Pn: ay-lee-oh-RAY-mus

54

Tarbosaurus

(Cr) Late
Cretaceous

Size: 46 ft (14 m) long
Order: Saurischia
Family: Tyrannosauridae
Range: Asia: Mongolia
Pn: TAR-boh-SAW-rus

Albertosaurus

Like all tyrannosaurs, *Albertosaurus* had a second set of ribs lining its belly. These extra ribs may have helped to support its insides so that they were not crushed by the animal's huge weight when it lay down. A fierce hunter, *Albertosaurus* could have killed its prey with a bite to the neck.

Albertosaurus

Tarbosaurus

Like all tyrannosaurs, *Tarbosaurus* had small, weak front limbs. There were two fingers on each hand, each bearing a claw. The legs and feet were large and bulky, with four toes on each foot. Three of these pointed forward and the fourth, much smaller, toe was directed backward. This fearsome creature could have driven other hunters away from their kills as well as hunting its own prey.

(Cr) Late
Cretaceous

Size: 26 ft (8 m) long
Order: Saurischia
Family: Tyrannosauridae
Range: North America: Alberta
Pn: al-BERT-oh-SAW-rus

Tyrannosaurus

Up to 20 feet (6 m) tall and weighing more than an African elephant, *Tyrannosaurus* was one of the most fearsome creatures of the Cretaceous. Some scientists think that its bulk may have made it hard for it to chase prey and believe that it scavenged for food, eating animals that were already dead. In fact, like lions today, *Tyrannosaurus* probably hunted and scavenged.

(Cr) Late
Cretaceous

Size: up to 49 ft (15 m) long
Order: Saurischia
Family: Tyrannosauridae
Range: North America: Alberta, Montana, Saskatchewan, Texas, Wyoming; Asia: Mongolia
Pn: tie-RAN-oh-SAW-rus

Tyrannosaurus

Feeding

What did dinosaurs eat? Like large animals today, many dinosaurs were plant eaters, although some would have hunted and killed other creatures. The largest hunters, such as *Tyrannosaurus*, could have hunted on their own. Smaller carnivores probably hunted in packs, attacking dinosaurs much larger than themselves. There were many more plant-eating dinosaurs than flesh eaters, but they could have avoided competition by feeding at different levels. Small dinosaurs, such as *Protoceratops*, would have grazed at ground level. Larger horned dinosaurs could have fed on low bushes, but had short necks and could not stretch up far. Hadrosaurs could have reared up on their hind legs to reach leaves higher in the trees. Biggest of all were the mighty sauropods, which could stretch up to eat the fresh growth at the tops of trees where no other creatures could reach.

Large horned dinosaur

Small horned dinosaur

Sharing resources

Here, a group of plant-eating dinosaurs, ranging from a small horned dinosaur to a giant sauropod feed together, each at its own level. The largest dinosaurs would have eaten huge quantities of plants every day to get enough nourishment. A sauropod might have eaten as much as 1 ton (1 tonne) of leaves a day.

Sauropod

The **fossilized droppings** of dinosaurs are known as coprolites and provide valuable clues about what dinosaurs ate. Coprolites that have been studied show the remains of conifer stems, cycad leaves, and flesh, for example. But although experts can tell what a dropping contains, it is hard to know to which species it belonged.

Fossilized droppings

Meat eater's skull

Skull structure

A plant eater, such as a duckbilled dinosaur, had a toothless beak at the front of the jaws that was used to chop mouthfuls of leaves. The food was then ground down on the tightly packed teeth farther back in the jaws. A meat eater, such as an allosaur, had powerful jaws lined with sharp teeth. These curved backward and had serrated edges for slicing into prey.

Hadrosaur

Plant eater's skull

Tyrannosaur

Mighty hunters

The largest hunters, such as tyrannosaurs, were built for power and strength. They had massive jaws and daggerlike teeth, which they could use to rip apart prey in seconds. Hunters may have had to spend time tracking down and catching prey, but one good meal could have satisfied them for several days.

57

Prosauropods

This group of long-necked dinosaurs first appeared in the Late Triassic. There were two main groups—the plateosaurids, which had large, heavy bodies, and the anchisaurids, which were smaller and more lightly built. Like the later sauropods, prosauropods are thought to have been plant eaters. Although these dinosaurs have some similarities to sauropods, they are not an early form of sauropod as their name suggests. They are probably a side branch of the group and they had died out by the end of the Early Jurassic.

Plateosaurus

Anchisaurus

A small, lightly built prosauropod, *Anchisaurus* had a small head, long neck and slender body. Its arms were shorter than its legs and it probably moved on two legs as well as four. On its thumb was a large claw, which the dinosaur may have used for uprooting plants or for defending itself.

J Early Jurassic

Size: 7 ft (2.1 m) long
Order: Saurischia
Family: Anchisauridae
Range: North America: Connecticut; southern Africa
Pn: AN-ki-SAW-rus

Anchisaurus

T Late Triassic **J** Early Jurassic

Size: 33 ft (10 m) long
Order: Saurischia
Family: Melanorosauridae
Range: South America: Argentina
Pn: ree-O-ha-SAW-rus

Riojasaurus

Riojasaurus

A large, bulky dinosaur, *Riojasaurus* was too heavy to rear up on to two legs. It would have had to walk on all fours in order to support its body weight. It is named after La Rioja Province in Argentina, where its fossils were found.

Plateosaurus

Many well-preserved skeletons of *Plateosaurus* have been discovered, making this the best known of the prosauropods. The tail made up about half the length of this large animal. It had a strong head and many small leaf-shaped teeth for feeding on plants. It would have moved on all fours for much of the time, but could have reared up on two legs to browse on the leaves of tall trees.

T Late Triassic

Size: up to 23 ft (7 m) long
Order: Saurischia
Family: Plateosauridae
Range: Europe: England, France, Germany, Switzerland
Pn: PLAT-ee-oh-SAW-rus

Lufengosaurus

J Early Jurassic

Size: 16–23 ft (5–7 m) long
Order: Saurischia
Family: Plateosauridae
Range: Asia: China
Pn: loo-FUNG-oh-SAW-rus

Lufengosaurus

Some 30 skeletons of this prosauropod have been discovered to date and *Lufengosaurus* was the first complete dinosaur to be mounted and displayed in China. It also appeared on the first ever dinosaur postage stamp, issued in China in 1958. A large, heavily built animal, *Lufengosaurus* had large hands, broad feet, and widely spaced teeth.

T Late Triassic

Size: 13 ft (4 m) long
Order: Saurischia
Family: Plateosauridae
Range: North America: Arizona; Africa: South Africa, Zimbabwe
Pn: MASS-oh-SPOND-ih-lus

Massospondylus

Mussaurus

In 1979 a group of tiny *Mussaurus* hatchlings were found in a nest in Argentina. Two small eggs lay nearby, each measuring only 1 inch (2.5 cm) long. Other skeletons found were about 12 inches (30 cm) long and probably belonged to young animals.

T Late Triassic   **J** Early Jurassic

Size: 7 ft (2.1 m) long
Order: Saurischia
Family: Anchisauridae
Range: Europe: England; southern Africa
Pn: THEEK-oh-don-toe-SAW-rus

Massospondylus

Massospondylus had a small head on a very long, flexible neck. Its large, five-fingered hands could have been used for collecting food or for walking when on all fours. Stones have been found with some skeletons—the dinosaur probably swallowed these to help it grind down tough plants in the stomach.

T Late Triassic   **J** Early Jurassic

Size: 10 ft (3 m) long
Order: Saurischia
Family: Plateosauridae
Range: South America: Argentina
Pn: moo-SAW-rus

Mussaurus

Thecodontosaurus

Like *Anchisaurus*, this dinosaur was lightly built, but it had a shorter neck and more teeth than its relative. It was first named in 1842 after its fossilized bones were found in southwest England.

Thecodontosaurus

59

Fossils

A fossil is the remains of an animal preserved in rock. Hard parts of the body, such as teeth, bones, and scales, are most likely to form fossils, but fossilized eggs and droppings have also been found. A fossil may also be formed of an imprint in the ground, such as a giant dinosaur footprint. Fossils only develop in certain conditions. Imagine, for example, that a dinosaur has died on a bank of a river or lake. The flesh is eaten by scavengers and insects, leaving only the bones, which slowly sink into the mud. Over the years, more and more mud piles up over the bones. Water filters down through the ground, carrying natural substances called minerals. These turn the mud and bones into rock. The skeleton keeps its shape but gradually changes into a fossil.

These fossilized dinosaur **footprints** were discovered in Utah. Footprints provide clues about how fast dinosaurs moved and whether they traveled in herds.

The teeth in this fossil of *Eudimorphodon,* one of the oldest flying reptiles, are particularly well preserved. Their shape would have been ideally suited to grasping slippery fish.

HOW A FOSSIL IS FORMED

1 Most of the dead dinosaur's flesh is eaten by carnivores or other scavenging reptiles and the rest soon decays.

2 The dinosaur's skeleton lies on the bed of the lake and sinks into the mud.

3 Over millions of years, more layers of lake sediment are deposited above the dinosaur skeleton.

4 The land has risen and erosion has started to remove some of the rock above the skeleton.

5 Finally, the last layers of rock are eroded to reveal the fossil bones.

Where fossils are found

Land over much of the world is covered by soil and plants. But in deserts, such as the arid regions of Utah (below), or where a great flood strips away the soil, rock is revealed and ancient bones may be seen once more. Even then, only part of a skeleton may be visible in a cliff face or an area of excavation.

Teeth fossilize well and can reveal much about the lifestyle of the owner. This long sharp tooth would have belonged to a meat-eating dinosaur.

Sauropods

These long-necked, plant-eating dinosaurs were the largest land animals ever known. The smallest were at least 33 feet (10 m) long and the largest may have measured as much as 125 feet (38 m). All were similar in appearance, with a small head on a long neck, a deep body, thick pillarlike legs, and a long tapering tail. They walked on all fours and were probably slow moving. There were several different families of sauropods. Brachiosaurs were some of the biggest and heaviest, while diplodocids, such as *Seismosaurus*, were even longer but had lighter bones.

Late Cretaceous

Size: 39 ft (12 m) long
Order: Saurischia
Family: Titanosauridae
Range: South America: Argentina
Pn: SALT-a-SAW-rus

Saltasaurus

Saltasaurus

Titanosaurs such as *Saltasaurus* first appeared in the Late Jurassic and survived until the end of the Cretaceous period. *Saltasaurus* was one of the smaller species. Set into its skin were a large number of small bony plates, some bearing spikes, which would have helped defend this plant eater against its flesh-eating enemies.

J Late Jurassic

Size: 49 ft (15 m) long
Order: Saurischia
Family: Camarasauridae
Range: Asia: China
Pn: yoo-HEL-oh-pus

Euhelopus

Euhelopus

Euhelopus was a close relative of *Camarasaurus,* although it lived on the other side of the world. Its body shape was very similar, but its neck was much longer and contained as many as 17 to 19 vertebrae. (*Camarasaurus* had only 12 vertebrae.) Its teeth were large and spoon shaped, suitable for eating tough plants such as ferns and horsetails.

Alamosaurus

Alamosaurus was one of the last titanosaurs and lived right at the end of the Late Cretaceous. Like others in its family, it had a broad snout with slender teeth that could have been used to strip leaves from branches. It is named after the Alamo, the famous fortress that the Texans held against a Mexican siege in 1836.

Cr Late Cretaceous

Size: 69 ft (21 m) long
Order: Saurischia
Family: Titanosauridae
Range: North America: Montana, New Mexico, Texas, Utah
Pn: AL-am-oh-SAW-rus

Barapasaurus

Barapasaurus

This sauropod is one of the oldest so far known. It had a typical sauropod body and some of the bones in its backbone and neck were hollow, lessening its weight. Six incomplete skeletons of this dinosaur have been found so far in southern India, but no skull.

J Early Jurassic

Size: 49 ft (15 m) long
Order: Saurischia
Family: Barapasauridae
Range: Asia: India
Pn: ba-RA-pa-SAW-rus

Cetiosaurus

Cetiosaurus

A huge creature with a shorter neck than most sauropods, *Cetiosaurus* may have weighed more than 9 tons (9 tonnes). When the first remains were discovered in 1809 people thought that the bones belonged to some giant sea creature—its name means "whale lizard."

J Middle to Late Jurassic

Size: 60 ft (18.3 m) long
Order: Saurischia
Family: Cetiosauridae
Range: Europe: England; Africa: Morocco
Pn: SEET-ee-oh-SAW-rus

Alamosaurus

Camarasaurus

Mighty *Camarasaurus* was one of the most common sauropods in Late Jurassic North America. Like other sauropods, it probably moved in herds and relied on its huge bulk to protect it from attack. An adult may have weighed 22 tons (20 tonnes).

J Late Jurassic

Size: 59 ft (18 m) long
Order: Saurischia
Family: Camarasauridae
Range: North America: Colorado, Oklahoma, Utah, Wyoming
Pn: kam-AR-a-SAW-rus

Camarasaurus

63

Diplodocus

J Late
Jurassic

Size: 85 ft (26 m) long
Order: Saurischia
Family: Diplodocidae
Range: North America: Colorado,
Montana, Utah, Wyoming
Pn: dip-LOD-oh-kus

Diplodocus

This huge animal's neck was 24 feet (7.3 m) long but, at only 24 inches (60 cm), its head was not much bigger than a horse's. Despite its size, *Diplodocus* weighed only 11 tons (10 tonnes), much less than *Brachiosaurus*. This was because its vertebrae were partly hollow. Its tail was made up of at least 70 bones and was probably held off the ground as it walked.

Brachiosaurus

Brachiosaurus

This giant may have weighed 88 tons (80 tonnes), more than 12 African elephants. Like a giraffe, it had a very long neck and front legs that were longer than its back legs so that the body sloped down from the shoulders. It probably fed like a giraffe, too, reaching up to eat leaves on the highest trees.

J Late
Jurassic

Size: 72 ft (22 m) long
Order: Saurischia
Family: Diplodocidae
Range: Asia: Mongolia
Pn: ma-MENCH-ih-SAW-rus

Mamenchisaurus

J Late
Jurassic

Size: 75 ft (23 m) long
Order: Saurischia
Family: Brachiosauridae
Range: North America: Colorado;
Africa: Tanzania, Algeria
Pn: BRACK-ee-oh-SAW-rus

J Late
Jurassic

Size: 125 ft (38 m) long
Order: Saurischia
Family: Diplodocidae
Range: North America: New
Mexico
Pn: SIZE-moh-SAW-rus

J Late Jurassic

Size: 41 ft (12.6 m) long
Order: Saurischia
Family: Diplodocidae
Range: Africa: Tanzania
Pn: die-KRAY-oh-SAW-rus

Dicraeosaurus

Dicraeosaurus

Dicraeosaurus was small compared to most members of its family and had a much shorter neck and larger head. Its name means "forked lizard" and comes from the forked spines that stuck out from its vertebrae. These may have helped to strengthen the backbone.

Mamenchisaurus

Mamenchisaurus had the longest neck of any animal known. It made up about half of the animal's total length and contained 19 extra-long vertebrae. Its long neck probably helped *Mamenchisaurus* reach fresh plant growth at the tops of trees.

Cr Early Cretaceous

Size: 33 ft (10 m) long
Order: Saurischia
Family: Diplodocidae
Range: South America: Argentina
Pn: a-MAR-ga-SAW-rus

Amargasaurus

Amargasaurus

This small diplodocid had two rows of spines growing up from its backbone. These may have helped to protect the dinosaur from predators. Or they may have been covered with skin to make a sail-like structure to help the dinosaur absorb or lose heat.

Apatosaurus

Although *Apatosaurus* would have moved on all fours, it may have been able to rear up on its back legs and bring its forelegs down to crush an enemy. Marks on the bones show that large muscles powered the tail, allowing the dinosaur to lash it from side to side to warn off attackers.

Seismosaurus

The remains of this sauropod, possibly the longest land animal ever, were first found by accident by two hikers in New Mexico. Its legs were short and thick to help support and steady its huge body, which may have weighed as much as 110 tons (100 tonnes).

Seismosaurus

Apatosaurus

J Late Jurassic

Size: 70 ft (21.3 m) long
Order: Saurischia
Family: Diplodocidae
Range: North America: Colorado, Oklahoma, Utah, Wyoming
Pn: a-PAT-oh-SAW-rus

Discovering dinosaurs

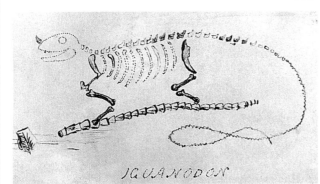

A sketch of *Iguanodon*, made by the British country doctor Gideon Mantell. He first discovered the remains of the dinosaur in 1822.

Most of what is known about dinosaurs comes from fossils, which may have lain untouched for millions of years. Sometimes fossils are found by chance, but usually they are uncovered by teams of dinosaur experts called paleontologists. Before the fossils are moved from their rocky bed, a detailed plan must be drawn, showing the position of each one. This may help the experts reconstruct the skeleton.

Once back in the museum, each bone is minutely examined for clues about the living animal. For example, tiny marks or roughened areas on the bone show where muscles were attached. Scientists also compare dinosaurs with similar creatures living today to work out how they may have looked and behaved.

A reconstructed skeleton of *Baryonyx*

Key

■ Fossil bones
□ Reconstructed bones

Rebuilding a skeleton

It is rare that a whole skeleton of a dinosaur or other creature is discovered. Usually missing parts have to be reconstructed using what knowledge scientists have of similar creatures. Only about 60 percent of the bones of the dinosaur *Baryonyx*, above and right, have ever been found.

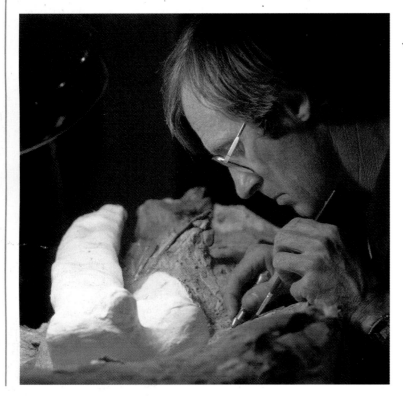

An **expert technician** painstakingly removes the fossilized ribcage of an *Albertosaurus* dinosaur from its plaster cast.

An artist's impression of what *Baryonyx* may have looked like

Digging for bones

When dinosaur bones, such as this tyrannosaur skeleton in Alberta, Canada, are found, they must be treated with the greatest care. The bones are freed from the surrounding rocks by paleontologists who use tools ranging from chisels and pickaxes to soft brushes. Then the bones are encased in a layer of sacking soaked in plaster of Paris. Once the plaster has hardened, the rock beneath the bones can be cut away and the whole section can be removed and taken to a museum laboratory for further investigation.

Boneheads and other plant eaters

Bonehead dinosaurs may have lived in herds much like the mountain goats of today. Like goats, they fed on plants and led peaceful lives for much of the time, but males probably fought fierce battles with rivals in the mating season. Much of the impact of their head-butting contests was taken by the tough bony dome on the head. Most bonehead fossils date from the Late Cretaceous and have been found in North America and central Asia. Like boneheads, fabrosaurs and heterodontosaurs were plant-eating dinosaurs and moved upright on long, slender legs.

Pisanosaurus

T Late Triassic

Size: 3 ft (90 cm) long
Order: Ornithischia
Family: Pisanosauridae
Range: South America: Argentina
Pn: pee-SAN-oh-SAW-rus

Lesothosaurus

Small and lizardlike, this fabrosaur had long legs, short arms, and a slender tail. It moved upright on its back legs and could probably speed across the African plains to escape from enemies. A plant eater, it had sharp, pointed teeth, shaped like little arrowheads, which it used to chop tough leaves.

Heterodontosaurus

Heterodontosaurus

Although similar to the fabrosaurs in appearance, *Heterodontosaurus* had quite different teeth. Unlike most other reptiles, it had three kinds—small pointed teeth like a mammal's incisors, which it used for nipping off leaves, larger back teeth for chewing, and two pairs of large canine teeth.

J Early Jurassic

Size: 3¼ ft (1 m) long
Order: Ornithischia
Family: Heterodontosauridae
Range: southern Africa
Pn: HET-er-oh-DONT-oh-SAW-rus

J Early Jurassic

Size: 3 ft (90 cm) long
Order: Ornithischia
Family: Fabrosauridae
Range: southern Africa
Pn: less-OH-toe-SAW-rus

Lesothosaurus

Cr Late Cretaceous

Size: 13 ft (4 m) long
Order: Ornithischia
Family: Pachycephalosauridae
Range: North America: Alberta
Pn: PAK-ee-KEF-a-loh-SAW-rus

Pisanosaurus

Few fossils have been found of this little dinosaur, but it may be one of the earliest of the ornithischian, or bird-hipped, dinosaurs. It lived during the Late Triassic period, millions of years before the other ornithischians appeared. It seems to have been lightly built and probably moved fast on its two back legs.

Pachycephalosaurus

The largest of the boneheads, this dinosaur had a huge dome on the top of its head made of solid bone, up to 10 inches (25 cm) thick. This dome probably acted like a crash helmet to protect the dinosaur's head when it took part in battles with rival males. The domes of males seem to have grown larger with age.

Pachycephalosaurus

Stegoceras

The thickened skull of *Stegoceras* was covered with lumps and knobs. When two males began a head-butting battle, they kept their heads lowered and neck, body and tail held straight out. The tail would have helped to balance the weight of the head.

Prenocephale

Like other boneheads, *Prenocephale* was a plant eater and probably fed on leaves and fruit. It walked on two legs and had five-fingered hands, three-toed feet, and a long heavy tail. The large dome on its head was surrounded with a row of bony spikes and bumps.

Stegoceras

Cr Late Cretaceous

Size: 6½ ft (2 m) long
Order: Ornithischia
Family: Pachycephalosauridae
Range: North America: Alberta
Pn: steg-O-ser-as

Cr Late Cretaceous

Size: 8 ft (2.5 m) long
Order: Ornithischia
Family: Pachycephalosauridae
Range: Asia: Mongolia
Pn: pren-oh-KEF-a-lee

Prenocephale

Cr Late Cretaceous

Size: 10 ft (3 m) long
Order: Ornithischia
Family: Homacephalidae
Range: Asia: Mongolia
Pn: home-ah-loh-KEF-ah-lee

Homalocephale

The homalocephalid family of boneheads did not have large domes on their heads. But the bones of the skull were heavy and thickened and the head was covered with bony knobs. *Homalocephale* also had unusually broad hips and some paleontologists believe that these took some of the impact when rival males fought.

Homalocephale

Hypsilophodonts

Hypsilophodonts were fast-running plant eaters, which probably lived in herds like deer today. When danger threatened, they could have escaped at high speed, running upright on their long, slender back legs. A highly successful group, hypsilophodonts lived from the Late Jurassic to the end of the Cretaceous. Fossils have been found so far in North America, Europe, Asia, Antarctica, and Australia. All members of the family had tall, grooved cheek teeth for grinding up plant food.

Parksosaurus

Cr Late Cretaceous

Size: 8 ft (2.5 m) long
Order: Ornithischia
Family: Hypsilophodontidae
Range: North America: Alberta
Pn: PARX-oh-SAW-rus

Hypsilophodon

At one time scientists believed that this dinosaur may have lived in trees— its body shape was thought to be similar to that of today's tree kangaroos. However, further study has shown that its feet are not suitable for grasping trees and that this animal was perfectly adapted for fast movement on land.

Hypsilophodon

Cr Early Cretaceous

Size: 5 ft (1.5 m) long
Order: Ornithischia
Family: Hypsilophodontidae
Range: North America: South Dakota; Europe: England, Portugal
Pn: hip-see-LOAF-oh-don

Parksosaurus

Parksosaurus was one of the last of the hypsilophodonts, surviving until the end of the Cretaceous. Although similar to its relatives, it had bigger eyes than most and had special bones to support its large eyeballs. *Parksosaurus* probably fed close to the ground, nipping off leaves with its narrow beaked jaws.

Dryosaurus

J Late Jurassic   **Cr** Early Cretaceous

Size: 10 ft (3 m) long
Order: Ornithischia
Family: Hypsilophodontidae
Range: western North America; Africa; Europe: England, Romania; possibly Australia
Pn: DRY-oh-SAW-rus

Dryosaurus

One of the largest of the hypsilophodonts, *Dryosaurus* was also one of the earliest. Like other members of its family, it had long legs that were built for speed, with shin bones that were much longer than its thigh bones. There were three toes on each of its slender feet.

70

Leaellynasaura

Fossils of this dinosaur were found in 1987 in the south of Australia. This region was once part of polar Gondwana, so the dinosaur must have been adapted to survive the long dark winters and freezing temperatures. Its eye sockets and the part of its brain devoted to vision were unusually large, suggesting that it had excellent sight.

Leaellynasaura

Cr Early Cretaceous

Size: 6½–10 ft (2–3 m) long
Order: Ornithischia
Family: Hypsilophodontidae
Range: Australia
Pn: LEE-el-in-a-SAW-ra

Thescelosaurus

Bulkier than most of its relatives, *Thescelosaurus* also had teeth in the front of its upper jaw. The structure of its legs, with shin bones and thigh bones of the same length, suggest that it was slower moving than other hypsilophodonts. But it did have rows of bony studs on its back that may have helped to protect it from enemies.

Othnielia

Othnielia

A typical hypsilophodont, *Othnielia* had long legs, a lightweight body, and short arms with five-fingered hands. Originally known as *Nanosaurus*, it was renamed in honor of the 19th-century American fossil collector Professor Othniel Charles Marsh to commemorate his work on dinosaurs.

J Late Jurassic

Size: 4½ ft (1.4 m) long
Order: Ornithischia
Family: Hypsilophodontidae
Range: North America: Utah, Wyoming
Pn: oth-ni-EL-ee-a

Cr Late Cretaceous

Size: 11½ ft (3.5 m) long
Order: Ornithischia
Family: Hypsilophodontidae
Range: North America: Alberta, Montana, Saskatchewan, Wyoming
Pn: thes-KEL-oh-SAW-rus

Thescelosaurus

Tenontosaurus

Tenontosaurus was much bulkier than most of its family and over half its length was made up of its heavy tail. It probably spent much of its time on all fours and it had longer arms than other hypsilophodonts. Daggerlike claws on its feet would have helped it defend itself from enemies.

Cr Early Cretaceous

Size: 24 ft (7.3 m) long
Order: Ornithischia
Family: Hypsilophodontidae
Range: North America: Arizona, Montana, Oklahoma, Texas
Pn: teh-NON-toe-SAW-rus

Tenontosaurus

71

Iguanodonts

Large, plant-eating dinosaurs, iguanodonts appeared in the Jurassic and spread all over the world. They were bulky, big-boned animals with sturdy legs and hooflike nails on their feet. Each short arm had a five-fingered hand, which could be spread wide and used for walking when on all fours. The thumb took the form of a spike that stuck out from the hand and could be used against attackers. Three of the other fingers bore hooflike nails and the small fifth finger could be bent across the palm of the hand and used for grasping food.

Vectisaurus

Vectisaurus

A close relative of *Iguanodon*, *Vectisaurus* lived at the same time and in the same area. The only difference between the two, apart from size, was that *Vectisaurus* had spines growing upward from its backbone that were long enough to form a definite ridge along the back.

Cr Early Cretaceous

Size: 13 ft (4 m) long
Order: Ornithischia
Family: Iguanodontidae
Range: Europe: England
Pn: VECK-ti-SAW-rus

Muttaburrasaurus

Found in Australia in 1981, fossils of this iguanodont show that it had a bony bump on its skull just in front of the eyes. No one knows exactly what this was used for but it could have been used in displays to attract mates.

Cr Early Cretaceous

Size: 24 ft (7.3 m) long
Order: Ornithischia
Family: Iguanodontidae
Range: Australia: Queensland
Pn: MUT-a-BUR-a-SAW-rus

Muttaburrasaurus

Ouranosaurus

Ouranosaurus had a row of spines running down the center of its back. These spines would have been covered with skin to form a finlike structure that may have helped the dinosaur control its temperature—when the fin was turned to the sun it would have absorbed heat.

Cr Early Cretaceous

Size: 23 ft (7 m) long
Order: Ornithischia
Family: Iguanodontidae
Range: Africa: Nigeria
Pn: OO-ran-oh-SAW-rus

Ouranosaurus

Iguanodon

Iguanodon

Iguanodon was the second dinosaur to be discovered—part of a leg bone was found in 1809 in southern England. Fossilized footprints suggest that *Iguanodon* lived in herds and was probably slow moving. It would have spent most of its time on four legs but could have reared up on two to feed on plants higher up.

Cr Early Cretaceous

Size: 30 ft (9 m) long
Order: Ornithischia
Family: Iguanodontidae
Range: Europe: Belgium, England, Germany; North America: Utah; Africa: Tunisia; Asia: Mongolia
Pn: ig-WA-no-don

Camptosaurus

An early member of the iguanodont family, *Camptosaurus* had four toes on each foot (other iguanodonts had three) and a poorly developed thumb spike. Like the rest of its family, this dinosaur had small hooves on its fingers and toes.

Probactrosaurus

Probactrosaurus

Like all iguanodonts, *Probactrosaurus* had a strong toothless beak for chopping mouthfuls of plant food. Farther back in the jaws were ridged teeth for grinding food down. New teeth grew as old ones wore out.

Cr Early Cretaceous

Size: 20 ft (6 m) long
Order: Ornithischia
Family: Iguanodontidae
Range: Asia: China
Pn: pro-BAK-trch-SAW-rus

Camptosaurus

J Late Jurassic

Size: 20 ft (6 m) long
Order: Ornithischia
Family: Iguanodontidae
Range: Europe: England, Portugal; North America
Pn: KAMP-toe-SAW-rus

Rhabdodon

When standing upright on their back legs, iguanodonts such as *Rhabdodon* would have held the long tail straight out behind to help balance the heavy weight of the body. This iguanodont lived on a group of volcanic islands located where central Europe is now.

Rhabdodon

Cr Early Cretaceous

Size: 13 ft (4 m) long
Order: Ornithischia
Family: Iguanodontidae
Range: Europe: France, Romania
Pn: RAB-doh-don

73

Family life

Like reptiles and birds today, most dinosaurs would have laid hard-shelled eggs in which their young grew. Although many fossil eggs have been found, few can be definitely identified as belonging to a particular species. Those that can be identified show that some dinosaurs looked after their eggs and young. In a nest belonging to *Troodon,* for example, eggs were arranged in a circle with the tips pointing neatly in toward the center. The nest also had a built-up rim surrounding it. One fossilized *Oviraptor* was found incubating its clutch.

The egg

A duckbilled dinosaur's egg was about 7 inches (18 cm) long and had a tough, waterproof shell to protect the growing baby inside. A newly hatched *Maiasaura* probably measured about 12 inches (30 cm). Fossils of leg bones show that the baby duckbill would have been too weak to move far and would have stayed in the nest for a few weeks being fed by its parents.

A caring mother

Fossilized eggs belonging to the duckbilled dinosaur *Maiasaura* (see page 77) were discovered arranged in circles in the middle of a nest mound. The mother probably lay next to the nest to guard her eggs from predators. Other remains of lots of little *Maiasaura* dinosaurs, all about the same age, show that the young were probably cared for in groups by a few adults while others went off to find food.

Battling boneheads

Dinosaurs such as boneheads (see pages 68–69) probably lived in herds. In the breeding season male boneheads may have fought fierce head-butting battles to win females or the leadership of the group. Some herding animals, such as mountain goats, do the same today.

This clutch of **fossilized eggs** belonging to *Oviraptor* was discovered in the Gobi Desert, Mongolia. Several such clutches have been found, some containing as many as 22 eggs.

Lambeosaurus

Corythosaurus

Parasaurolophus

Hypacrosaurus

Duckbilled dinosaur crests

Keeping in touch

Fossilized tracks and finds of groups of bones show that many types of plant-eating dinosaurs lived in herds. Like plant eaters today, they would have found that moving in herds helped to protect them from predators. Duckbilled dinosaurs, or hadrosaurs, may have made special calls to keep in touch with others in their herd, as well as to attract mates. The differently shaped crests on the duckbills may have acted as echo chambers to help make the calls louder. The crests may also have helped the dinosaurs recognize others of their own species. Females may have had smaller crests than males.

Duckbilled dinosaurs

Also known as hadrosaurs, duckbilled dinosaurs get their name from their long, flattened beak. One of the largest and most varied of Late Cretaceous dinosaur groups, hadrosaurs were particularly common in North America and Asia. All had long back legs and shorter front legs. They probably spent much of their time on all fours while feeding but could rear up on their back legs to run away from attackers. They are thought to have lived in herds and nested in groups. Although some hadrosaurs had flat heads, many had a strangely shaped crest on the top of the head.

Anatosaurus

Cr Late Cretaceous

Size: 33 ft (10 m) long
Order: Ornithischia
Family: Hadrosauridae
Range: North America: Alberta
Pn: an-at-oh-SAW-rus

Anatosaurus

Two "mummified" bodies of *Anatosaurus* dinosaurs have provided rare clues to their diet. The stomach contents include pine needles, twigs, seeds, and fruit. Like other hadrosaurs, it may have stood up on its back legs to gather food from trees.

Edmontosaurus

Like all hadrosaurs, *Edmontosaurus* had a toothless beak for cropping plants. Behind this, in both upper and lower jaws, were as many as a thousand tightly packed teeth for grinding down the food. As teeth became worn they were replaced with new ones. The neck was strong yet bendy, allowing the dinosaur to gather low-growing plants from a wide area around it, without having to move.

Shantungosaurus

One of the biggest hadrosaurs known, *Shantungosaurus* had a particularly long tail, measuring up to almost half the total body length. Deep and flattened in shape, the tail was held out behind to help balance the body weight when the dinosaur walked upright. *Shantungosaurus* may have weighed as much as 5 tons (4.5 tonnes).

Bactrosaurus

Bactrosaurus

This is the earliest known duckbilled dinosaur. The group appeared in the Late Cretaceous at the same time as flowering plants spread throughout the world. This plentiful food supply—and their efficient plant-grinding jaws for making use of it—may have been the reason for the great success of the duckbills.

Cr Late Cretaceous

Size: 13 ft (4 m) long
Order: Ornithischia
Family: Hadrosauridae
Range: Asia: Mongolia and China
Pn: bak-troh-SAW-rus

Cr Late Cretaceous

Size: 43 ft (13 m) long
Order: Ornithischia
Family: Hadrosauridae
Range: Asia: China
Pn: shan-TUNG-oh-SAW-rus

Edmontosaurus

Hadrosaurus

Cr Late Cretaceous

Size: 43 ft (13 m) long
Order: Ornithischia
Family: Hadrosauridae
Range: North America: Alberta, Montana
Pn: ed-MON-toh-SAW-rus

Hadrosaurus

This duckbill was the first dinosaur to be discovered in North America. Its bones were found in New Jersey and it was reconstructed and named in 1858. Like *Kritosaurus*, *Hadrosaurus* was a flat-headed duckbill. It had no crest but there was a large hump made of bone on its snout.

Cr Early Cretaceous

Size: 30 ft (9 m) long
Order: Ornithischia
Family: Hadrosauridae
Range: North America: Montana, New Jersey, New Mexico, South Dakota
Pn: HAD-roh-SAW-rus

Kritosaurus

No one knows exactly why flat-headed dinosaurs such as *Kritosaurus* had bony humps on their snouts. It is possible that only the males had humps and that they used them in courtship displays.

Maiasaura

Cr Late Cretaceous

Size: 30 ft (9 m) long
Order: Ornithischia
Family: Hadrosauridae
Range: North America: Montana
Pn: my-ah-SAW-rah

Maiasaura

The discovery of a complete *Maiasaura* nest site in Montana proved that dinosaurs were social animals. The females nested in groups and may even have returned to the same site year after year like turtles and many birds today. It is possible that the dinosaurs also shared the care of the young, some remaining on guard while others fed.

Kritosaurus

Shantungosaurus

Cr Late Cretaceous

Size: 30 ft (9 m) long
Order: Ornithischia
Family: Hadrosauridae
Range: North America: Alberta, Montana, New Mexico
Pn: KRITE-oh-SAW-rus

Protohadros

Protohadros

Discovered in Texas, which would have been covered with marshland at the time, *Protohadros* is the oldest, most primitive duckbill known. The fact that it was found in the United States means that duckbills may not have first evolved in Asia as scientists previously believed.

Cr Late Cretaceous

Size: up to 20 ft (6 m) long
Order: Ornithischia
Family: Hadrosauridae
Range: North America: Texas
Pn: pro-toe-HAD-ross

Saurolophus

The face of this duckbill curved upward from its broad snout to the tip of the bony crest on the top of the head. A fleshy nose sac, which helped make the dinosaur's calls louder, may have been attached to the crest.

Saurolophus

Cr Late Cretaceous

Size: 30 ft (9 m) long
Order: Ornithischia
Family: Hadrosauridae
Range: North America: Alberta, California; Asia: Mongolia
Pn: SORE-oh-LOAF-us

Parasaurolophus

Cr Late Cretaceous

Size: 30 ft (9 m) long
Order: Ornithischia
Family: Hadrosauridae
Range: North America: Alberta, New Mexico, Utah
Pn: par-a-SORE-oh-LOAF-us

Parasaurolophus

A spectacular, backward-pointing crest, more than 6 feet (1.8 m) long, topped the head of this dinosaur. The crest was hollow inside and may have acted like an echo chamber to make the dinosaur's booming calls louder. When the dinosaur held its head up, the crest may have fitted into a small notch in the backbone.

Tsintaosaurus

A tall horn grew from the top of this duckbill's head. It pointed straight up from between the eyes and had a notched tip. There has been much disagreement among experts about the position and use of this horn. Some think there may have been a flap of skin attached that was used like a flag for signalling to other members of the herd or in courtship rituals.

Prosaurolophus

Corythosaurus

A spectacular fan-shaped crest crowned the head of this duckbill. Crests of several different sizes have been found. Smaller crests may have belonged to young animals or females.

Cr Late Cretaceous

Size: 26 ft (8 m) long
Order: Ornithischia
Family: Hadrosauridae
Range: North America: Alberta
Pn: PRO-sore-oh-LOAF-us

Prosaurolophus

This duckbill had a low crest of bone running from the tip of the flat snout up to the top of the head. It ended in a small bony knob. Like all duckbills, *Prosaurolophus* had a toothless beak at the front of its head for gathering plant food.

Corythosaurus

Cr Late Cretaceous

Size: 30 ft (9 m) long
Order: Ornithischia
Family: Hadrosauridae
Range: North America: Alberta, Montana
Pn: ko-RITH-oh-SAW-rus

Lambeosaurus

Lambeosaurus

Like all members of its family, *Lambeosaurus* would have moved about on all fours as it fed. But if threatened, it could probably rear up on its back legs to run away. It had two structures on its head—a tall hollow crest at the front and a solid bony spike pointing backward.

Cr Late Cretaceous

Size: 30 ft (9 m) long
Order: Ornithischia
Family: Hadrosauridae
Range: North America: Baja California, Montana, Saskatchewan
Pn: LAM-bee-oh-SAW-rus

Hypacrosaurus

Hypacrosaurus had a semicircular crest on its head similar to that of *Corythosaurus*. This duckbill also had tall spines along its back—these probably formed a skin-covered ridge. The ridge may have helped it control its body temperature—when turned to the sun the ridge could absorb heat.

Cr Late Cretaceous

Size: 9 m (30 ft) long
Order: Ornithischia
Family: Hadrosauridae
Range: North America: Alberta, Montana
Pn: hie-PAK-roe-SAW-rus

Tsintaosaurus

Cr Late Cretaceous

Size: 33 ft (10 m) long
Order: Ornithischia
Family: Hadrosauridae
Range: Asia: China
Pn: SIN-tow-SAW-rus

Hypacrosaurus

Stegosaurs

Stegosaurs were large, plant-eating dinosaurs. A typical stegosaur had a small head, huge body, and heavy tail, lined with long sharp spikes. The most extraordinary features of these dinosaurs were the rows of large triangular plates on the back. There are several different ideas about their use, but many experts believe that they helped to control body temperature. The plates may have been covered with skin rich in blood vessels. When the stegosaur turned toward the sun, its blood would have been warmed as it passed through the plates. When the animal turned away from the sun or into a breeze, the plates would have lost heat, so cooling the body.

Scutellosaurus

This dinosaur was an early form of stegosaur. Lining its back and sides were rows of bony studs that may have helped to protect the animal from attackers. Its tail was about half its total length and could have been held out to balance the weight of the body when the dinosaur ran on two legs.

Scutellosaurus

Tuojiangosaurus

This Chinese stegosaur had a small narrow head and a heavy body. Its back was lined with 15 pairs of bony plates, which were taller and spikier toward the hips. The long spikes on the tail could have been used as a weapon against attackers. *Tuojiangosaurus* was the first stegosaur to be found in Asia.

J Late Jurassic

Size: 23 ft (7 m) long
Order: Ornithischia
Family: Stegosauridae
Range: Asia: China
Pn: toh-HWANG-oh-SAW-rus

Tuojiangosaurus

Wuerhosaurus

Only a few bones and plates have been found belonging to this dinosaur so no one knows exactly how it looked. *Wuerhosaurus* was one of the few stegosaurs to have survived into the Early Cretaceous—the group began to die out toward the end of the Jurassic period.

Cr Early Cretaceous

Size: 20 ft (6 m) long
Order: Ornithischia
Family: Stegosauridae
Range: Asia: China
Pn: WER-oh-SAW-us

Wuerhosaurus

Stegosaurus

One of the largest and best known stegosaurs, *Stegosaurus* had a double row of bony plates on its back, some measuring up to 24 inches (60 cm) high. The heavy tail was armed with spikes up to 3¼ feet (1 m) long.

J Early Jurassic

Size: 4 ft (1.2 m) long
Order: Ornithischia
Family: Scelidosauridae
Range: North America: Arizona
Pn: skoot-EL-oh-SAW-rus

Scelidosaurus

Lexovisaurus

Some experts believe that the bony plates on stegosaurs were not used for controlling body temperature but for helping the dinosaurs recognize their own species and attract mates. The arrangement of plates and spines was different in each species. *Lexovisaurus* had two rows of large thin plates.

J Middle Jurassic

Size: 16 ft (5 m) long
Order: Ornithischia
Family: Stegosauridae
Range: Europe: England
Pn: lex-OH-vi-SAW-rus

Scelidosaurus

One of the earliest ornithischian dinosaurs, *Scelidosaurus* may have been an early form of stegosaur. It had a small head, a toothless beak, and little teeth that were set farther back in its jaws. Its heavy body was covered in bony plates, studded with rows of spikes running from the neck to the tail.

J Early Jurassic

Size: 13 ft (4 m) long
Order: Ornithischia
Family: Scelidosauridae
Range: Europe: England
Pn: skel-ID-oh-SAW-rus

Lexovisaurus

Kentrosaurus

Stegosaurus

J Late Jurassic

Size: 30 ft (9 m) long
Order: Ornithischia
Family: Stegosauridae
Range: North America: Colorado, Oklahoma, Utah, Wyoming
Pn: STEG-oh-SAW-rus

J Late Jurassic

Size: 16 ft (5 m) long
Order: Ornithischia
Family: Stegosauridae
Range: Africa: Tanzania
Pn: KEN-tro-SAW-rus

Kentrosaurus

Smaller than *Stegosaurus*, *Kentrosaurus* was almost as well armored with bony plates and spikes. If attacked, the stegosaur could lash out with its spiked tail and wound its attacker. Long spikes at hip level provided extra protection against enemies.

Cretaceous times

The biggest change that took place during the Cretaceous period, which began 146 million years ago, was the appearance of the first flowering plants. Small herbs, bushes, and deciduous trees took over from horsetails and cycads and became the dominant greenery on the Earth. There was more plant food than ever, allowing huge herds of plant eaters, such as horned dinosaurs and duckbills, to thrive. With flowering plants came pollinating insects and many more species of mammals and birds.

Pteranodon, a flying reptile (pterosaur)

Magnolia

Cretaceous North America

In this scene in what is now Montana, a duckbill dinosaur bellows her alarm as she returns to her nest to find an agile *Troodon* stealing her eggs. Lizards and an early mammal scuttle by, while a tyrannosaur stalks nearer to a group of feeding horned dinosaurs.

Sycamore

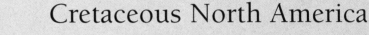

Albertosaurus, a tyrannosaur

Small mammal

Centrosaurus, a horned dinosaur

Lizard

Moss

Troodon

The Cretaceous world

In the Cretaceous, the world's landmasses continued to drift apart until by the end of the period they were close to their positions today. The climate was generally warm and there were greater differences between the seasons. As the land broke into smaller pieces, greater differences between the dinosaurs in different continents developed as they evolved in isolation from each other.

Montana

North America

Europe

Asia

ATLANTIC OCEAN

Turkey

PACIFIC OCEAN

TETHYS OCEAN

South America

Africa

India

Australia

Antarctica

Corythosaurus

Key to map

Ocean

Landmass

Sea-covered continent

Conifer

Early oystercatcher

Troodon, a bird relative (maniraptoran)

Corythosaurus, a duckbilled dinosaur

Lizard

Armored dinosaurs

Two groups of heavily armored dinosaurs were common in the Cretaceous period—nodosaurs and ankylosaurs. In both, the neck, back, sides, and tail were covered with flat plates of bone, set into the thick leathery skin. Nodosaurs had narrow skulls and long spikes that stuck out at the sides of the body. Ankylosaurs had broader skulls and a heavy ball of bone like a club at the end of the tail. If attacked, an ankylosaur could swing this from side to side and cause severe damage to its attacker. The broad-snouted ankylosaurs probably ate any low plants they could find, whereas the nodosaurs, with their narrower muzzles, may have selected certain leaves.

Panoplosaurus

Cr Late Cretaceous

Size: 15 ft (4.5 m) long
Order: Ornithischia
Family: Nodosauridae
Range: North America: Alberta, Montana, South Dakota, Texas
Pn: pan-o-ploe-SAW-rus

Panoplosaurus

This heavily armored nodosaur had broad plates of bone across its neck and shoulders while the rest of the back was covered in smaller bony studs. Huge spikes guarded each side and even the head was protected with thick pieces of bone.

Euoplocephalus

Cr Late Cretaceous

Size: 18 ft (5.5 m) long
Order: Ornithischia
Family: Ankylosauridae
Range: North America: Alberta
Pn: you-op-loh-KEF-ah-lus

Euoplocephalus

Like other ankylosaurs, this dinosaur had a heavy bony club at the end of its tail that could have weighed more than 60 pounds (27 kg). Powerful muscles at the hips helped *Euoplocephalus* swing its clubbed tail from side to side against any attacker.

Hylaeosaurus

Cr Early Cretaceous

Size: 20 ft (6 m) long
Order: Ornithischia
Family: Nodosauridae
Range: Europe: England
Pn: hy-lee-oh-SAW-rus

Hylaeosaurus

Hylaeosaurus was one of the earliest dinosaurs to be described and named. A fossil was found in southern England in the 1820s by Gideon Mantell, one of the first ever dinosaur experts. The bones are still imprisoned in the block of limestone in which they were found but the creature is believed to be a nodosaur.

Saichania

Like most ankylosaurs, *Saichania* had a network of air passages inside its skull. These may have helped to cool or moisten air before it reached the dinosaur's lungs. This was important because Mongolia at this time was hot and humid, but with very dry spells.

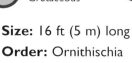

Cr Late Cretaceous

Size: 16 ft (5 m) long
Order: Ornithischia
Family: Ankylosauridae
Range: Asia: Mongolia
Pn: tal-a-ROO-rus

Talarurus

Talarurus

Like all armored dinosaurs, *Talarurus* ate plants, which it cropped with the toothless beak at the front of its jaws. The club on the end of its tail was made from two large balls of bone joined together. Thin bony rods strengthened the tail to support the heavy club.

Cr Late Cretaceous

Size: 23 ft (7 m) long
Order: Ornithischia
Family: Ankylosauridae
Range: Asia: Mongolia
Pn: sy-KAHN-ee-a

Saichania

Sauropelta

This tanklike creature is the largest known nodosaur. It may have weighed as much as 3 tons (2.7 tonnes). Bony, horn-covered plates protected its back, and sharp spikes stuck out from each side. Its bulk made *Sauropelta* slow moving, but its armor would have put off all but the most determined predators.

Polacanthus

Few fossils of this dinosaur have been found, but it is thought to have had large spines protecting its shoulders and tail. Smaller spiny plates guarded the sides and a mass of bone covered the hips. Like other nodosaurs, it may have crouched down when attacked, relying on its armor for defense.

Cr Early Cretaceous

Size: 13 ft (4 m) long
Order: Ornithischia
Family: Nodosauridae
Range: Europe: England
Pn: pol-a-KAN-thus

Cr Early Cretaceous

Size: 25 ft (7.6 m) long
Order: Ornithischia
Family: Nodosauridae
Range: North America: Montana
Pn: SAW-roh-PEL-ta

Sauropelta

Polacanthus

85

ARMORED DINOSAURS

Horned dinosaurs

There were three main groups of horned dinosaurs. First came the "parrot dinosaurs," or psittacosaurs, of the Early Cretaceous. These lightly built dinosaurs had distinctive parrotlike beaks. In the Late Cretaceous came the protoceratopids, which had heavier bodies and the beginnings of the bony neck frills that developed so dramatically in the later ceratopsians. The ceratopsians were the most common large plant eaters in Late Cretaceous western North America. These well-armored dinosaurs had long sharp horns on their massive heads and a bony frill at the back of the neck.

Bagaceratops

Cr Late Cretaceous

Size: 3¼ ft (1 m) long
Order: Ornithischia
Family: Protoceratopidae
Range: Asia: Mongolia
Pn: BAG-a-SER-a-tops

Bagaceratops

This little protoceratopid had a squat body and long tail, supported on four solid legs. At the back of its neck was a bony ridge and there was a short horn halfway along its snout. Unlike other members of its family, it had no teeth in its upper beak.

Microceratops

Microceratops

Cr Late Cretaceous

Size: 24 in (60 cm) long
Order: Ornithischia
Family: Protoceratopidae
Range: Asia: China, Mongolia
Pn: mik-roh-SERRA-tops

The smallest horned dinosaur known, *Microceratops* was lightly built and was probably a fast runner. Its shin bones were almost twice as long as its thigh bones—a sign of a speedy dinosaur. It may have moved on all fours as it fed on plants, rising up on two legs to escape from danger.

Psittacosaurus

A parrotlike toothless beak covered with horn is the reason for this dinosaur's name, which means "parrot lizard." This dinosaur fed on plants, which it cropped with its strong beak. It had bony ridges on the sides of its head but no neck frill like the later ceratopsians.

Psittacosaurus

Cr Early Cretaceous

Size: 8 ft (2.5 m) long
Order: Ornithischia
Family: Psittacosauridae
Range: Asia: China, Mongolia, Siberia
Pn: si-TAK-oh-SAW-rus

Montanoceratops

Although it had a definite horn on its snout, *Montanoceratops* was a protoceratopid, not a member of the more advanced ceratopsian family. Its tail was unusually deep and flexible and could probably have been moved rapidly from side to side. The tail may have been used as a courtship signal in the mating season or as a way of recognizing its own species.

Leptoceratops

This was one of the few protoceratopids to be found in North America. Most of the family lived in Asia. Its back legs were built for running and it could probably move on four legs or two. The five-clawed fingers on its hands could have been used for picking leaves and passing them to the mouth.

Cr Late Cretaceous

Size: 7 ft (2.1 m) long
Order: Ornithischia
Family: Protoceratopidae
Range: North America: Alberta, Wyoming; Asia Mongolia
Pn: LEP-toe-SER-a-tops

Leptoceratops

Protoceratops

When fully grown this dinosaur probably weighed almost 400 pounds (180 kg). An impressive creature, it had a large bony neck frill at the back of its heavy head and powerful beaked jaws. It had a large bump on its snout that may have been used in fights between rival males.

Protoceratops

Cr Late Cretaceous

Size: 9 ft (2.7 m) long
Order: Ornithischia
Family: Protoceratopidae
Range: Asia: China, Mongolia
Pn: PRO-toe-SER-a-tops

Montanoceratops

Cr Late Cretaceous

Size: 10 ft (3 m) long
Order: Ornithischia
Family: Protoceratopidae
Range: North America: Montana
Pn: mon-tan-oh-SERRA-tops

Chasmosaurus

This horned dinosaur had a huge bony neck frill that stretched from the back of the skull to cover its neck and shoulders. A spectacular frill like this could have been used to warn off enemies as well as to attract females.

Cr Late Cretaceous

Size: 17 ft (5.2 m) long
Order: Ornithischia
Family: Ceratopsidae
Range: North America: Alberta
Pn: KAZ-mo-SAW-rus

Chasmosaurus

Anchiceratops

This horned dinosaur lived near the end of the Late Cretaceous and was slightly more streamlined than some of its relatives. Its body was longer and its bony neck frill narrower. Like other horned dinosaurs, it fed on plants, which it gathered with its sharp, toothless beak.

Anchiceratops

Cr Late Cretaceous

Size: 20 ft (6 m) long
Order: Ornithischia
Family: Ceratopsidae
Range: North America: New Mexico
Pn: PEN-ta-SER-a-tops

Triceratops

One of the largest and most common horned dinosaurs, *Triceratops* weighed as much as 10 tons (9 tonnes). Its skull alone was more than 6 feet (1.8 m) long. Like others in its family, *Triceratops* probably lived in large herds. Rival males may have fought one another, locking horns and pushing with their head shields.

Cr Late Cretaceous

Size: 20 ft (6 m) long
Order: Ornithischia
Family: Ceratopsidae
Range: North America: Alberta
Pn: AN-ki-SER-a-tops

Pentaceratops

Pentaceratops

Like *Chasmosaurus*, this horned dinosaur had a huge neck frill, which was fringed with small spines. There were several large openings in the bony surface to make the frill lighter. The name of this dinosaur means "five-horned face" because scientists thought it had horns on its cheeks as well as on its snout. In fact, these were just elongated cheek bones.

Cr Late Cretaceous

Size: 30 ft (9 m) long
Order: Ornithischia
Family: Ceratopsidae
Range: North America: Alberta, Colorado, Montana, Saskatchewan, South Dakota, Wyoming
Pn: try-SER-ah-tops

Triceratops

Torosaurus

Torosaurus

The skull of this dinosaur is one of the largest known of any land animal, living or extinct. Including the enormous neck frill, which extended from the back of the head, it measured more than 8 feet (2.5 m). With this and the three pointed horns on its snout, *Torosaurus* was a challenge for any predator.

Cr Late Cretaceous

Size: 25 ft (7.6 m) long
Order: Ornithischia
Family: Ceratopsidae
Range: North America: Montana, South Dakota, Texas, Utah, Wyoming
Pn: TOR-oh-SAW-rus

Pachyrhinosaurus

The skulls that have been found suggest that *Pachyrhinosaurus* had no horns on its snout. Instead, it had a thick bony pad just above the eyes. This may have protected the head, like the thickened skull of boneheads (see pages 68–69), or may simply have marked the place where the horns had fallen off.

Pachyrhinosaurus

Cr Late Cretaceous

Size: 18 ft (5.5 m) long
Order: Ornithischia
Family: Ceratopsidae
Range: North America: Alberta
Pn: PAK-ee-RINE-oh-SAW-rus

Styracosaurus

Styracosaurus

The amazing bony neck frill of this horned dinosaur had an array of sharp spikes around the edge. With these and its great nose horn, *Styracosaurus* could have defended itself against attackers by charging toward them with head held down, just like a rhinoceros today.

Cr Late Cretaceous

Size: 17 ft (5.2 m) long
Order: Ornithischia
Family: Ceratopsidae
Range: North America: Alberta, Montana
Pn: sty-RAK-oh-SAW-rus

Centrosaurus

Like other horned dinosaurs, *Centrosaurus* had thick pillarlike legs with heavy bones to support the bulky body. The short wide toes were fanned out to help spread the weight. Despite the size of its head and bony neck frill, a mobile neck joint ensured that *Centrosaurus* could turn its head quickly and easily.

Cr Late Cretaceous

Size: 20 ft (6 m) long
Order: Ornithischia
Family: Ceratopsidae
Range: North America: Alberta, Montana
Pn: SEN-troh-SAW-rus

Centrosaurus

89

Why did the dinosaurs disappear?

No one knows exactly what caused the mass extinctions that destroyed many of the Earth's creatures, including the dinosaurs, 65 million years ago. Some scientists believe that the dinosaurs may have been becoming less numerous a few million years before the final extinction. The drop in numbers could have been caused by the cooler climate that resulted from the many volcanic eruptions at the time. Other experts believe that the extinctions were caused by the impact of a massive meteorite that hurtled down from space.

What died and what survived?

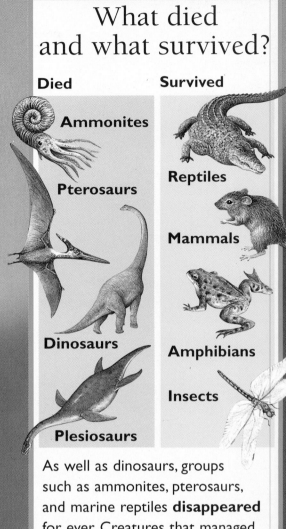

Died	Survived
Ammonites	Reptiles
Pterosaurs	Mammals
Dinosaurs	Amphibians
Plesiosaurs	Insects

As well as dinosaurs, groups such as ammonites, pterosaurs, and marine reptiles **disappeared** for ever. Creatures that managed to survive the mass extinction included other kinds of reptiles, such as crocodiles, lizards, and snakes, as well as mammals, amphibians, and insects.

Meteorite impact?

A meteorite (above), measuring at least 6 miles (10 km) across, may have struck the Earth at the end of the Cretaceous period and caused the death of the dinosaurs and other creatures. Huge amounts of debris thrown up by the impact would have darkened the skies for many years, causing a long cold period and the death of plants. Plant-eating dinosaurs would have soon starved to death, followed by the meat eaters that fed on them. The evidence for this theory includes the discovery of a vast crater near the north coast of Mexico (right) that could have been caused by a huge impact. Another important piece of evidence is the fact that rocks of that time all over the world contain minerals that could have come from a meteorite.

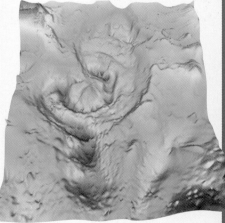

▲ This computer-generated image shows the meteorite crater now underwater and buried under a deep layer of rock. The blue area at the bottom of the picture shows the channel made by the meteorite as it landed.

Volcanic eruptions

Even a small volcanic eruption can cause local climate change, and in the Late Cretaceous there was an enormous amount of volcanic activity. These eruptions would have thrown huge quantities of ash and dust into the air, causing the climate to change and destroying plants and animals.

Volcanic eruptions that took place in the Deccan region of India at the end of the Cretaceous period caused a massive outpouring of lava. The lava formed the layers of rock now known as the Deccan Traps (above). They prove that there were extraordinary events on the Earth at this time that may have caused the death of the dinosaurs.

This scene in the area now known as Montana shows the effect of increased **volcanic activity** on the wildlife of the time. Debris has darkened the sky and blocked out sunlight. Plants are dying and with them plant eaters. Meat eaters manage to survive for a while by scavenging.

Quetzalcoatlus, a flying reptile (pterosaur)

▼Dromaeosaurus, a bird relative (maniraptoran) feeding on Edmontosaurus, a duckbilled dinosaur

Edmontonia, an armored dinosaur

Triceratops, a horned dinosaur

Pachycephalosaurus, a bonehead dinosaur

Glossary

amphibian A four-legged vertebrate animal that can live on land and in water but usually lays its eggs in water. Modern amphibians include frogs, toads, and salamanders.

archosaur The group of reptiles to which dinosaurs and pterosaurs belonged. Crocodiles are the only surviving archosaurs.

Aves The name of the order to which birds belong.

billion One thousand million.

Carboniferous The period from 360 to 290 million years ago.

carnivore An animal that eats the flesh of other animals in order to survive.

club moss A type of plant that lived before flowering plants and was most common in the Triassic and Jurassic. Club mosses were common in the Carboniferous period but are now almost extinct.

Cretaceous The period from 146 to 65 million years ago.

cycad A type of cone-bearing plant that lived before flowering plants. Cycads had short thick trunks and long palmlike leaves.

evolution The gradual development of species of plants and animals through time. As plants and animals develop, or evolve, their characteristics change.

extinction The complete dying out of a type of plant or animal.

family A group of related species. For example, all the species of duckbilled dinosaurs, such as *Maiasaura*, belong to the family Hadrosauridae. The scientific name of a family usually ends in -idae.

fossil The remains of an animal preserved in rock. Bones and teeth are more likely to form fossils than soft body parts. Impressions in mud, such as footprints, can also be fossilized.

Gondwana An ancient landmass formed when Pangaea broke up about 180 million years ago. Gondwana split to form the southern landmasses of South America, Africa, India, Australia and Antarctica.

Jurassic The period from 208 to 146 million years ago.

Laurasia An ancient landmass formed when Pangaea broke up about 180 million years ago. Laurasia then split to form the northern landmasses of North America and Eurasia.

mammal A four-legged vertebrate animal that has hair on its body and feeds its young on milk produced in its own body. Mammals include animals such as cats, horses, and humans.

mass extinction The disappearance of a large number of different species over a short period of time.

meteorite A lump of rock from outer space that enters the Earth's atmosphere and lands on Earth.

order An order is a group of related families. For example, there are two orders of dinosaurs: the Ornithischia and the Saurischia. Some large orders are divided into smaller suborders.

Ornithischia One of the two orders of dinosaurs. The orders differ in the structure of their hip bones (see pages 40–41). All ornithischians fed on plants.

paleontologist A scientist who specializes in the study of fossils and ancient life.

Pangaea An ancient continental landmass that formed about 240 million years ago and included all the world's land. It later split into two parts – Gondwana and Laurasia.

Permian The period from 290 to 250 million years ago.

predator An animal that hunts and kills other animals for food.

prey An animal hunted by a predator.

reptile A four-legged vertebrate animal that lays eggs with tough, leathery shells. Dinosaurs, pterosaurs, and ichthyosaurs were all reptiles. Modern reptiles include tortoises, snakes, lizards, and crocodiles.

Saurischia One of the two orders of dinosaurs. The orders differ in the structure of their hip bones (see pages 40–41). Saurischians included plant-eating and meat-eating dinosaurs.

scavenger A creature that feeds on the remains of animals that have died naturally or been killed by other flesh eaters.

species A term for a type of plant or animal. Members of the same species can mate and produce young that can themselves have young.

theropod A meat-eating dinosaur.

Triassic The period from 250 to 208 million years ago.

vertebra One of the bones that make up a backbone. The backbone is made up of a number of vertebrae.

vertebrate An animal with a backbone. Mammals, birds, reptiles, amphibians, and fish are all vertebrates.

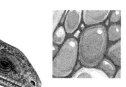
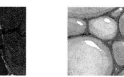

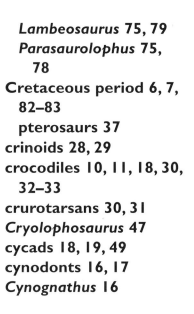

Milleretta

Index

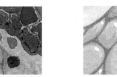

94

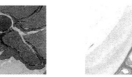 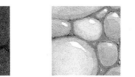 

List of abbreviations

Metric
cm = centimeters
m = meters
km = kilometers
km/h = kilometers per hour
km² = square kilometers
kg = kilograms

Imperial
in = inches
ft = feet
mph = miles per hour
sq miles = square miles
lb = pounds

Iguanodons

Acknowledgments

Photographic credits
t = top; b = bottom

3 E.R. Degginger/Oxford Scientific Films; 8–9 Ken Lucas/Planet Earth Pictures; 12 Peter Menzel/Science Photo Library; 28 Dr R. Wild/Staatliches Museum für Naturkunde Stuttgart; 36 The Natural History Museum, London; 38–39 Pat Morris/Ardea; 40 François Gohier/Ardea; 42 Mary Evans Picture Library; 57 The Natural History Museum, London; 60t François Gohier/Ardea, 60b Specimen: Museo Civico di Scienze Naturali "E. Caffi" Bergamo, Italy/Dr R. Wild; 60–61 Jules Cowan/Bruce Coleman; 61 The Natural History Museum, London; 66t The Natural History Museum, London, 66b Paul A. Souders/Corbis; 67 Jonathan Blair/Corbis; 75 The Natural History Museum, London; 91 E. Hanumantha Rao/NHPA

Artwork credits
t = top; b = bottom; c = center; r = right; l = left

Artists:
3–5 Steve Kirk; 5b Peter David Scott/Wildlife Art Agency; 6 Eugene Fleury; 6–7tc Roger Stewart; 7Steve Kirk; 9 Steve Kirk; 10t Peter David Scott/Wildlife Art Agency; 10b Steve Kirk; 11 Steve Kirk; 12–13 Martin Sanders; 14–17 Steve Kirk; 18–19 James Field/Simon Girling Associates; 19t Eugene Fleury; 20–29 Steve Kirk; 29t Elizabeth Gray; 30–37 Steve Kirk; 36b Elizabeth Gray; 39 Steve Kirk; 40 Peter David Scott/Wildlife Art Agency; 41tc Elizabeth Gray; 41b Peter David Scott/Wildlife Art Agency; 42–43 Martin Sanders; 44–47 Steve Kirk; 48–49 James Field/Simon Girling Associates; 49t Eugene Fleury; 50–55 Steve Kirk; 56–57 Peter David Scott/Wildlife Art Agency; 57br Steve Kirk; 58–59 Steve Kirk; 61t Guy Smith/Mainline Design; 62–73 Steve Kirk; 74t Robin Bouttell/Wildlife Art Agency; 74b Peter David Scott/Wildlife Art Agency; 75t Peter David Scott/Wildlife Art Agency; 75b Steve Kirk; 76–81 Steve Kirk; 82–83 James Field/Simon Girling Associates; 83t Eugene Fleury; 84–89 Steve Kirk; 90–91 David Bergen/Virgil Pomfret Agency; 90tr Peter David Scott/Wildlife Art; 90cl David Bergen/Virgil Pomfret Agency; 92–95 Steve Kirk.